FINDING FAMILY

*My Search for Roots
and the Secrets in My DNA*

RICHARD HILL

This book is dedicated to my wife, Pat. If she had not pushed me, I would never have started this search. And without her unwavering support, I could never have finished it.

FOREWORD

No discussion of an adoptee's personal history can be complete without a careful investigation into whom his or her biological parents were and why he or she was given up for adoption.

There are at least seven million adopted children and adults in the US today. Knowing that a number of diseases are at least partly genetic, many of those children pass into adulthood wondering what health risks they inherited.

Consciously or not, adoptees also deal with many more emotionally charged questions. What is my ethnic background? Do I have brothers or sisters? Do they look like me? What were their lives like? Are they aware that I exist? And if so, might they or my birth parents now be searching for me?

In this fascinating, inspirational, and highly personal account, Richard Hill brings all these issues front and center. I found myself wondering what new facts would be found on the next paragraph and page of this personal odyssey to find the truth surrounding the circumstances of his birth and adoption.

Combining conventional genealogy, DNA analysis, and good old-fashioned gumshoe detective work, Richard has weaved his personal story into a thrilling saga that should serve as a roadmap for anyone seeking the "who" and "why" of an adoptee's birth.

Although Richard's quest was ultimately successful, you'll see the journey was neither easy nor quick. Dogged persistence trumps luck when searching for an adoptee's biological family and this journey is filled with moments of euphoria separated by weeks, months, and years of frustration.

Written in an easy-to-read style, Richard Hill's book is a guide for adoptees seeking answers to questions that have been covered (purposely or otherwise) by the sands of time. He has demonstrated that persistence and patience are the best tools for the adoptee looking to uncover the secrets to his or her biological beginnings.

As the president of Family Tree DNA, the world largest genealogical site employing DNA to prove connections, I see many adoptees every week struggling with the same questions that Richard has worked to answer in this book. My hope is that by reading about his journey, other adoptees also will obtain the closure that Richard sought, and found, after more than thirty years of investigation.

BENNETT GREENSPAN
PRESIDENT
FAMILY TREE DNA

INTRODUCTION

This is a true story. The names, places, and dates are all real. The people responsible for my successful outcome are too numerous to list. But you will meet them on the following pages.

Without their individual contributions, the many mysteries surrounding my birth never would have been completely solved.

For adoptees and countless others uncertain of their parentage, this book can be an essential guidebook of tips and techniques.

The early part of my search predated the Internet. And genetic genealogy DNA tests only became available in the later stages of my story. But the many human factors involved in a successful search for lost family members are timeless.

Science buffs and social scientists should be intrigued at the way DNA testing has opened doors for adoptees and others to overcome sealed records and decades-old family secrets.

Finally, anyone who enjoys a good mystery or human-interest story is invited to accompany me on the roller coaster ride of my life.

RICHARD HILL
Grand Rapids, Michigan

To know who you are, you have to know where you came from.

—WHO DO YOU THINK YOU ARE?
TELEVISION SERIES

1

REVELATION

All families have secrets, some bigger than others.

My family's secret leaked out in 1964, the year I graduated from high school. The place was Ionia, Michigan, a small town halfway between Lansing and Grand Rapids.

It was late August and a strange pain in my chest was keeping me awake at night. Since our longtime family doctor had retired, I made an appointment with Dr. Campbell, who now had my medical file.

He quickly identified my problem as acid reflux. Heartburn. Thinking stress was the cause, he began to question me about my life.

Ionia is a small town and Dr. Campbell had seen my picture in the local newspaper. Remembering that I graduated second in my class, he asked if I felt pressure to perform well in school.

"No," I replied honestly.

He asked if I was nervous about going away to college.

Again, I said "No." Living on campus would be a new adventure and I looked forward to it with genuine eagerness.

As Dr. Campbell thumbed through my medical file, I wondered what his next question would be. There was no way for me to guess—or to be prepared for—what he asked me next.

"How do you feel about being adopted?"

My heart skipped a beat.

"Excuse me?" I asked. I must have misheard him. Or maybe he had me confused with someone else. I'm Richard Hill, son of Harold and Thelma Hill. Surely, he must have someone else's file in his hands.

When Dr. Campbell saw my stunned reaction, he looked mortified.

"I'm sorry. I...I just assumed you knew," he stammered. The expression on his face suggested he was now the one feeling a jolt of stomach acid. He had inadvertently let slip what we both knew was a life-altering secret.

My mind raced.

Why hadn't my parents told me? They loved me. Of that, I had no doubt. Yet, why did they intentionally withhold a piece of information this crucial?

We talked it over for a few minutes. Dr. Campbell tried to assure me that my parents chose to adopt me and would love me like any parents love their child. I said I understood. But I didn't. Not really. I wondered why they had kept me in the dark about this.

Nevertheless, I was on break from my summer job at Hub Shoe Store and had to get back to work. There wasn't time for a lengthy analysis. So he wrote a prescription to help with my heartburn. Then he made me promise to call him if my symptoms did not improve or if I just needed to talk. I knew he was worried about how I would react.

In a daze, I walked the short block back to the store. Fortunately, it was a Friday and I would be working until 9 p.m. I had a lot of time to reflect on this revelation before going home to face my parents.

As I half-heartedly waited on customers, my mind picked up pieces from the bombshell that had exploded in the doctor's office.

My old family doctor must have been part of a conspiracy that included my parents and others. The secret only slipped out because my medical records fell into the hands of an outsider. Had my old doctor not retired when he did, I never would have discovered the truth.

In another week, this window of opportunity would have closed forever. I would have been living on campus where health center doctors could not browse my childhood medical file.

The author and his adoptive parents

Adopted? Me?

I began to search for clues I must have missed. No, I didn't look out of place in my family. My parents and I all had dark-brown hair. In fact, my Dad and I both had hair so dark it was nearly black.

In the last couple of years, I had sprouted up to six feet four inches in height. So I was much taller than my five-foot, nine-inch father and my five-foot, two-inch mother. But many of my high school friends were taller than their parents. Hadn't I read somewhere that this was due to my generation's better diet and health care?

One clue I might have caught, but didn't, was the fact that my parents were a lot older than most of my friends' parents. Dad was forty years old when I was born and Mom was thirty-four. That was odd, but apparently not strange enough to sound an alarm. I had never given it much thought. But now it seemed clear they spent a long time trying to have children before deciding to adopt.

Now that I thought about it, just being an only child was a little unusual back then. Most of my friends had at least one sibling. But like the age clue, it wasn't exactly a neon sign.

As the store traffic slowed, I had a flashback to tenth-grade biology.

Our textbook had used eye color as an example of how parents' DNA recombines in a child. Brown is dominant and blue is recessive. So two blued-eyed parents should only produce blue-eyed children.

Both of my parents had blue eyes. Mine are light brown. Puzzled by the apparent impossibility of my family's eye colors, I had approached my biology teacher after class. Mrs. Stewart explained that the eye-color example was a simplification. For one thing, it ignored eye colors like green and gray.

She went on to explain that scientists did not understand all the genes controlling our physical traits. Plus, there was always the possibility of a mutation that didn't follow the rules.

Since I was sure of my parents back then, I concluded I was a mutant. This was actually rather cool. Having grown up with Superman, Green Lantern, and other comic book heroes, I briefly wondered how else I was different.

Biology class then moved ahead to sexual reproduction, which we teenagers found a lot more interesting than the abstractions of DNA. I forgot about the eye color discrepancy and never mentioned it to my parents.

But here I was, a couple years later, with an entirely new perspective. My parents' blue eyes now struck me as absolute proof of my adoption.

I wondered. Had my biology teacher given me an honest answer? Or was she also part of this conspiracy to conceal the truth?

That conspiracy, I deduced, must have included my aunts and uncles and my parents' best friends. My grandparents would have been in on it, too, but they were all gone by then.

I wondered if my cousins knew. Two of them were roughly twenty years older than I was. They must have noticed that their Aunt Thelma had never looked pregnant in the months before my birth.

The rest of my cousins, however, were either younger than I or no more than a year older. None of them had ever mentioned my adoption, so I assumed they didn't know.

I would have years to speculate on these things. But I only had a few hours to make one critical decision: what was I going to say to my parents when I got home that night?

2

MOVING ON

By the time we locked up the store, I knew the answer. Learning about my adoption did not make any real difference in my life. Harold and Thelma Hill were still the only parents I knew. They loved me. And I loved them.

The fact that I was an only child eliminated a potential sore spot. I could never say they played favorites and treated a biological child better than they treated me.

I was disappointed they had not told me the truth. But I assumed they had their reasons. I also knew that my leaving home for college in a few days was going to be difficult for them. So this seemed like a poor time to make an issue of my adoption.

Besides, I reasoned, they might just be waiting for the right time to tell me, perhaps when I turned twenty-one. In the meantime, if they didn't want to talk about my adoption, I would not mention it either.

Looking back, this unexpected news arrived at the perfect time for me to accept it gracefully. So close to starting college, my focus was entirely on my future. The details of my past did not seem so important right then.

By the age of eighteen, I was also mature enough to deal with the news more logically than emotionally. Had the secret slipped out when I was younger, the shock might have damaged my self-image or my relationship with my adoptive parents.

On the other hand, not knowing earlier about my adoption had spared me from the psychological issues that plague many adoptees in childhood and adolescence. Clearly, my family and I were lucky.

When I arrived home that evening, I greeted my parents as I always did: we exchanged hellos and I inquired about their day. Since I had called the doctor's office from the store phone, they were unaware of my appointment. I chose not to mention it and acted as though nothing had changed.

That wasn't true, of course. In a way, everything had changed.

I had lived in Ionia most of my eighteen years and knew hundreds of people. Yet every familiar face now triggered the same unspoken questions: Did they know I was adopted? Were they part of the conspiracy to hide the truth? Or were they as ignorant as I had been?

As planned, I moved to East Lansing and began my life as a Michigan State Spartan. I loved the big, beautiful campus and the magic surrounding football games in the fall. In my junior year, I witnessed the famous 10-10 tie with Notre Dame from a seat on the forty-yard line.

In addition to dating, partying, and watching football, I somehow found time to study. My major was physics and I received my BS in June 1968.

The job market was strong that year and I received seven job offers, mostly in East Coast metropolitan areas. But I also had one from out West. And when I saw the beautiful mountains of northern New Mexico, I chose to work at the Los Alamos Scientific Laboratory (now called the Los Alamos National Laboratory).

Another deciding factor was the escalating war in Vietnam. With my student deferment ending, working at a lab that did weapons work ensured an occupational deferment. In 1968, that benefit was more valued than health insurance and vacation time.

In the two weeks between graduation and moving out West, I squeezed in one other thing: I got married.

I had met Pat Franich two summers before at the Crystal Lake Palladium. Known for its quarter-acre dance floor, it had been a popular stop for the big bands of the 1940s. Now it was a gathering place for the under-twenty-one crowd on summer weekends. Pat was from Ithaca, an even smaller town, more than an hour's drive from Ionia.

Raised on her family's farm, Pat had gone to beauty school and began her career as a hairdresser. By the fall of 1966, she had already switched careers and was working in an office in Lansing. Fortunately for both of us, she was living in an East Lansing apartment not far from the MSU campus. We dated my last two years in college and timed our wedding for the Saturday after graduation.

I told Pat about my adoption and explained how my family still thought I was unaware of it. When she met my parents, she played dumb, too.

Naturally, I did wonder about my biological parents. Mom's favorite movie was *Gone with the Wind*. I thought I could see myself in Clark Gable. For many years, I had a fantasy that I was the secret love child of Clark and some gorgeous actress.

After Sonny and Cher appeared on television, I learned that Cher and I shared the same birth date: May 20, 1946. Like her, I was slender with dark hair. So my new fantasy had me being Cher's twin brother, somehow separated at birth.

Adoption is inherently a two-sided coin. On one side, there is gratitude that a nice family chose to raise you as their own. On the flip side, there's a sense of loss. Your birth parents had to give you up for this to happen.

Fortunately, the emotional coin landed heads up for me. I only felt the positive side of adoption.

If I did have any unanswered questions about my identity, I was able to compartmentalize them and get on with my life. As the years slipped by, any inclination to discuss the matter with my parents evaporated.

Near the end of our five-year stay in New Mexico, Pat and I became parents. Our first child, Jennifer, was born there in March 1973. She was the first blood relative I ever saw.

When Jenny was six months old, I followed through on a career decision I had been contemplating for nearly two years. I resigned my position at the lab and went back to MSU to get a master's degree in business.

Family considerations were partly behind the move. My dad had suffered a severe heart attack while I was still in college. Unable to pass his employer's physical, he never returned to work. That heart condition had kept him from accompanying Mom when she came out to visit us in New Mexico. His doctor insisted that the 7,300-foot altitude of Los Alamos would be dangerous to his health.

Now that Pat and I had a child, we wanted grandparents to be part of her life. So we moved back to East Lansing for my stint in grad school. Beyond that, we hoped to remain in Michigan.

The economy was down when I received my MBA in 1975. But I was able to land a job in Grand Rapids with Lear-Siegler as director of marketing for its new Automated Systems Division. Happily, Pat and I bought our first house in the Grand Rapids suburbs, less than an hour from Ionia.

We saw my parents a lot over the next couple of years and they proved to be excellent grandparents. Jenny adored her "Nana" and "Grampy" and they adored her.

Since his heart attack, Dad had lived with the possibility of sudden death. Enjoying each day to the fullest, he was mentally prepared to die. Therefore, it was a cruel turn of events when he suffered a massive stroke in February 1977. Instead of providing the quick death he had anticipated, the stroke left one side of his body paralyzed.

Not quite seventy-one years old, Dad would spend the rest of his life bedridden. After some time in the Ionia Hospital, he transferred to Kent Community Hospital in Grand Rapids, a long-term care facility. I got in the habit of visiting him during my lunch hour several times a week. I would bring my brown bag lunch and we would talk about family, friends, weather, my work, and more.

Knowing that her husband was never coming home, Mom sold their home and moved into a senior citizen apartment in Ionia. She drove to Grand Rapids for regular visits with Dad. But she saw him at different times than I did to give Dad more visits. We almost never saw him at the same time.

Dad had been quite active in retirement. He loved to fish and would tie his own flies and mend fly rods for friends. A longtime member of the Elks Club, he enjoyed playing cards and pool with his pals. Late in life, he took up coin collecting, met often with other collectors, and traveled around the state to coin shows.

In the moment of that stroke, all of his hobbies were gone.

Dad also had been an avid reader. But the stroke damaged his vision to the point where he could not read, even with glasses. We bought him a thirteen-inch color TV that fit on his bed tray. But he still had a lot of time to just lie there and think.

In his solitary reflections, he must have agonized about the lifelong secrecy surrounding his only child. At some point, he reached a decision on what he had to do.

3

ANOTHER SHOE DROPS

During one of my lunchtime visits in January 1978, Dad suddenly brought up the subject of my adoption. He said something no one else had figured out or at least dared to say:

"By now, you must know you're adopted."

I was almost thirty-two years old and had not thought about my adoption for many years. So his statement caught me by surprise. I just smiled and acknowledged that I had known for a long time. He didn't ask how I knew or when I found out. So I just listened to what he wanted to say.

I already knew I had been born at St. Lawrence Hospital in Lansing. My parents had lived in Lansing because Dad worked at the Oldsmobile Forge Plant as a tool and die maker. Mom, a licensed cosmetologist, ran a beauty shop.

Originally from Ionia, they returned to their hometown when I was still a baby. They once told me Lansing was too big a city for raising a child. So for all the years I could remember, Dad commuted seventy miles a day driving to and from the Olds plant on the west side of Lansing.

My out-of-town birth must have made it easier to pass me off as their biological child. Close friends and family would know the truth. But it would have been easy to fool casual acquaintances.

Knowing what little I did about adoption, I assumed some social agency had placed me anonymously. I never dreamed my adoptive parents would know anything about my biological mother. I could not have been more wrong.

On this day when Dad broke his silence, he shocked me first by telling me that he and Mom had met my biological mother. He described her as a "cute little Irish girl" whose name was Jackie. She was young, under twenty-one, and from the Detroit area.

Her family knew Mildred, nicknamed Mickey, and Wayne Woods, a Lansing couple who were close friends of my parents. Wayne, in fact, had worked with Dad at Oldsmobile.

Then Dad surprised me with even more details: Jackie had actually lived with him and my mother in their Lansing apartment for the final months of her pregnancy. After my birth in May 1946, my new parents brought me directly home from the hospital and Jackie returned to Detroit.

Dad made a point to mention that he paid the hospital bill for my delivery. I think he was proud of taking responsibility for me from day one.

This revelation was another shock. I had known unwed mothers from my high school who quietly left town before their pregnancies showed. But it never occurred to me that a young woman could live with the same people who were going to adopt her child. That seemed to violate the whole secrecy thing that I had assumed was always part of the adoption process.

Ironically, I thought, the openness of my pre-birth arrangements may have created the need for secrecy after my birth. Unlike most adoptive parents, mine could not claim ignorance about my birth mother. They would not want to lie to me. Yet they would not want me tracking her down, either.

They were probably right. If I had had this information earlier, I would have pressured Wayne and Mickey for answers. But by the time Dad revealed their role, those two links to my birth mother were deceased.

I asked Dad if he ever heard anything more about Jackie in the years after my birth. He then told me that she had died in a car accident not long after my birth, but he couldn't remember exactly when or where.

Now that Dad had finally talked to me about my adoption, I could see the relief in his eyes and hear it in his voice. Carrying around that big secret for decades must have been an enormous burden.

My mother, of course, had no idea that Dad and I were having this conversation. She still believed the family secret was safe.

I guessed that Dad wanted to get the whole thing off his chest before he went to meet his maker. And I was happy for both of us. But he wasn't done. He had one more surprise to lay on me.

Since the stroke had also affected Dad's brain, there were days when I wasn't the only one in his room who was "out to lunch." But on the day of this conversation, Dad was clear and lucid as he gave me the rest of the story.

"When you were born, Jackie was divorced. She already had a son from her marriage. So you have a brother."

I was sure the nurses outside Dad's room must have heard the noise my jaw made as it hit the floor. I had been raised an only child and except for my whimsical fantasy about Cher, I never expected to have any siblings.

That part of the story blew away more preconceived ideas about adoption. I assumed all unwed mothers were school-age girls too young to get married. Many would marry later and have other children with their husbands. Somehow, in a way I couldn't quite grasp, my biological mother had managed to accomplish the whole feat backwards.

Dad went on to say that I deserved to know about my brother. I agreed and thanked him for sharing that information. Yet this revelation wasn't just about sharing. In all his lonely hours of contemplation, he had settled on a far bigger purpose than merely telling me the facts. I will never forget his next words:

"I think you should find your brother."

4

NO TIME. NO WAY.

When I got home that night, I told Pat about my conversation with Dad. She was intrigued and asked me how I felt knowing some details about my biological family. I joked that it ruined my fantasies. Clearly, the cast of characters in my adoption story did not include Clark Gable or Cher.

Seriously, though, it did feel good to have some answers. I never dreamed I would get any answers at all, let alone the surprising details that Dad had shared with me.

The idea of having a brother was exciting. Being an only child can be lonely, especially when your father isn't around much.

Dad worked the 3:30 to midnight shift with an hour's commute before and after. On weekdays, he was asleep when I got up and he would leave for work before I returned from school. That left Mom and me alone five nights a week and I wasted a lot of evenings just watching TV.

If I had grown up with a brother, I thought, we could have played catch, just hung out, or created a little mischief.

This, of course, was a fantasy. You can't turn back time. Even if I found my brother next week, my childhood was gone and so was his. Our relationship would have to be as adults with families, jobs, and responsibilities.

For the first time, I felt a little anger. My parents knew my birth mother and, with their silence, kept me from meeting her. They also knew I had a brother and—until Dad spilled the beans—kept me from knowing he even existed.

Now it was too late to meet my birth mother. She was dead. And with Wayne and Mickey Woods also deceased, it might be too late to connect the dots to my brother.

But maybe all was not lost.

I knew Wayne and Mickey had a daughter, Carol, who was a year ahead of me in school. But she grew up in Lansing and I had not seen her since high school. By now, she would probably be married and no longer known as Carol Woods. Plus, Carol was a baby herself when I was born. Would she know anything about someone named Jackie from Detroit who died while Carol was a child?

I guessed there could be other ways to track down Jackie's family. But no matter which path I took, a search would require a lot of my time. And in 1978, free time was in short supply.

My job with Lear-Siegler had required extensive travel. And all that time away from home made me realize the importance of family and how much I missed mine.

So nine months earlier I had left Lear-Siegler for a job with its advertising agency, Alexander Marketing Services, a small, local company specializing in industrial and technical clients. It was a job that made better use of my talents, paid better, and most importantly, required almost no overnight travel.

When Dad gave me the tantalizing clues about my biological family, I was still trying to learn the ad agency business and the products and markets of the clients I supported. That left precious little time to begin a search for my biological roots.

Then there was the not-so-little issue of Pat's pregnancy. By the time of Dad's revelation, she was seven months along and had already gained more weight than she had when Jenny was born. A recent ultrasound explained the weight gain. We were going to have twins in March.

Twice more during our lunchtime talks, Dad asked me if I had found my brother. Each time I explained that it would be a difficult search with Wayne and Mickey gone and I was currently too busy to tackle it. He seemed to understand.

Meanwhile, I continued to massage Dad's story in my mind. I was pleased that my adoptive parents had been part of my life from the very beginning. Avoiding foster care or time in an orphanage probably explained why I had bonded so well with my new family.

I was also fortunate that Jackie had been under my adoptive mother's supervision for much of her pregnancy. The fact that Mom would not have allowed an underage girl to smoke or drink alcohol on her watch may have saved me from some horrible birth defect.

In February, a year after his stroke, Dad's health insurance benefits ran out. The only remaining option for a bedridden stroke patient was a nursing home. To make it easier for Mom to visit him, we chose the one in Ionia.

In March, our boy-girl twins were born as scheduled. Wanting to avoid twin-like monikers, we named them Mark and Catherine. Naturally, a lot of sleepless nights followed, and since Pat's mother and stepfather were living in Florida, my mother was the only grandparent available to help with the new babies. We could not have survived without her.

We wanted Dad to see his new grandchildren. But the nursing home would not allow them inside. Fortunately, it was a one-story building. So once the weather got better, Pat held the twins in the yard outside Dad's room while I pointed him toward the window. He had seen pictures. But seeing them in person—even through a window—was better.

Mark and Catherine would never get to know their grandfather. Dad promptly got pneumonia and his doctor had him moved to the Ionia Hospital. The prognosis was grim. Mom stayed with him all day and I took over in the evenings.

It was May 1978. Mom and I agreed that after fifteen months of a bedridden, paralyzed existence, it was time to let him go. The hospital staff understood and posted a "Do Not Resuscitate" sign on his door.

On that last evening, Dad could not talk or open his eyes. So I don't know if he heard me. But I held his hand and thanked him for being a good father. A little while later, he simply stopped breathing. I kissed him good-bye and notified the nurse.

I was thankful that Dad had chosen to reveal the family secret before he died. But Mom did not know about Dad's revelation and I had still not pursued the clues he gave me.

This time it wasn't a focus on my future that kept me from exploring my past. With two new babies and a new career, it was the unrelenting demands of the present.

5

LIGHTING THE FIRE

By the fall of 1981, the twins were three years old and Jenny was eight. The hectic years of double feedings, double diapering, and double everything had passed. But all the distractions had snuffed out my desire to search for my biological family. Something had to light a fire in me.

It was Pat's cousin, Pam, who provided the spark.

I did not know Pam well. She was living in California and I'd only met her a couple times. But a personal mission brought her to our home that fall. As a young woman, Pam had gotten pregnant and given up her baby for adoption. An agency in Grand Rapids had placed her son with his adoptive parents and the boy was about to turn eighteen.

Unable to have other children, Pam longed to meet the boy she gave away. She was in town to search for him.

After Pam told us her adoption story, Pat told her mine. When Pam learned I had a brother and some clues about my birth mother, she practically screamed at me.

"You've got to find him!"

Pat agreed with her and the two of them would not relent until I agreed to start my search.

I knew that Michigan, like most states, had a policy of sealing adoption records. Even as an adult, an adoptee may not see the most fundamental records of his existence.

Pam explained that the sealed files are kept by the probate court in the county where the adoption took place, in my case Ingham County. The court will, if requested, provide adoptees with what they call non-identifying information.

On November 12, 1981, nearly four years after Dad's revelations, I took the first step of my search. Following Pam's suggestion, I wrote to the Ingham County Probate Court to request my non-identifying information.

I also placed an order with the state health department for my birth certificate. I did not expect them to send me the real one. But I was curious to see what I would get.

Pam also told me about a group called the Adoption Identity Movement (AIM) that met monthly in a suburban library. I marked the next AIM meeting date on my calendar.

Secretly, I wondered if I would regret starting this search. The phrase "opening a can of worms" would surely apply here. Where would this lead? Would there be a happy ending? Or a sad one?

Two factors gave me the courage to proceed. First, my science education taught me to seek the truth, whatever it was. And second, I knew I was both adaptable and resilient. I had already survived dramatic career changes, cross-country moves, the arrival of twins, and the loss of my father. So I felt confident that I could handle a simple search into my background.

Wondering what I could do before the AIM meeting, I decided to discreetly contact some people who had to know about my adoption.

Discretion was required because of my mother. She still had not opened the subject and apparently intended to take the secret to her grave.

If she knew I was searching for my biological family, I was certain she would jump to the conclusion that I didn't love her. That wasn't true, of course. I was not looking to replace the family that loved and raised me. I was just looking for information.

Still, not wanting to cause her any pain, I asked each contact not to mention my inquiry.

I began by dropping in on my cousin, Jim, who lived in Ionia. Twenty-three years older than I was, Jim joined the Navy before I was born and served in World War II. His kids were about my age and he was like a favorite uncle.

Jim and his wife, Donna, were happy to help. They had met my birth mother, Jackie, when she lived in the Lansing apartment with my soon-to-be adoptive parents. Donna remembered that my mother had put Jackie to work washing hair in her beauty shop.

Jim remembered Jackie as short, attractive, and under twenty-one. My mother told them later that Jackie had died. The accident occurred not long after I was born—maybe a year. Neither had heard anything specific about my biological father. Yet they somehow got the impression he was a "professional man."

When I got home, I called my Aunt Irene in Lansing. She knew about Jackie but had not met her in person. If Jackie had died in an accident, she did not remember hearing about it.

Irene did confirm that my adoption was indeed a closely guarded secret. She remembered my grandmother burning papers and letters relating to it.

These early, cooperative responses got me excited. If I just contacted the right people, maybe I could solve this mystery quickly.

My next thought was to call Dr. Campbell, the one who had accidentally revealed my adoption seventeen years earlier. Perhaps there was additional information in my medical file.

By this time, the doctor had retired to Arizona. But I knew his son from high school and got the phone number from him. Dr. Campbell did remember me. In fact, he joked that he would never forget the unique incident that took place in his office.

The doctor had no first-hand information about my birth mother. But he had heard a rumor not long after our talk. He promised to check with the source and call me back. After a short wait, my phone rang and Dr. Campbell relayed the following story:

My father was a doctor in Lansing, a prominent specialist who looked a lot like me. The doctor was married and my mother had been a nurse or a student nurse when she got pregnant. At the time Dr. Campbell heard the rumor, my mother was supposedly some kind of professor or instructor at Michigan State.

I asked if I could talk to the person who told him this. But his contact did not want to get involved and had made him promise not to reveal his or her identity. Dr. Campbell phrased his remarks carefully, so I couldn't even tell if his source was a man or a woman.

A doctor certainly fit Jim and Donna's recollection that my father had been a professional man. And I liked the thought of my father being a prominent specialist. If he couldn't be Clark Gable, maybe a brain surgeon would be a nice alternative.

But this story didn't fit at all with what I was hearing from others. If my birth mother had been living in Detroit, how would she have had an affair with a Lansing doctor? If she had died in an accident shortly after my birth, how could she have become a college professor?

If this story were true, my birth mother would have taught at MSU during my undergraduate years. I could have walked right by her on campus. And my birth father would have lived and worked somewhere right around me in the Lansing area. The possibilities were fascinating.

After hanging up with Dr. Campbell, I tracked down the wife of a high school classmate who worked as a nurse at a Lansing hospital. I asked her if she could think of any specialists that looked similar to me. No one came to mind.

My next call was to Dorothy Kanouse. She and her husband had been lifelong friends of my parents, so she had to know something. I learned that Dorothy had met my birth mother twice during the months that Jackie lived with my parents. Dorothy and her husband had jokingly referred to the Lansing apartment as "Thelma's Incubator."

She guessed Jackie's age to be eighteen or nineteen and remembered her having dark hair. Dorothy was right there at St. Lawrence Hospital the day I was born. She was reasonably certain that my birth mother never saw me.

24

Dorothy also had heard about a fatal accident involving Jackie. She even remembered some details. It was a Jeep with four passengers on board.

Now I had two totally conflicting scenarios to research. In one, my birth mother died young. In the other, she might still be alive. There was no question in my mind that I needed to pursue both possibilities until one or the other proved to be false.

6

DEAD OR ALIVE?

Was my birth mother, Jackie, dead or alive?

Believing that every cloud has a silver lining, I found advantages in each alternative. If Jackie were alive, the advantages were obvious. I might still be able to meet her. She could explain why she gave me up for adoption and I could learn the identity of my biological father.

Finding the silver lining in her death required a little more thought. Having spent months with my adoptive parents, Jackie knew enough about their family and friends to find me someday, just like Pat's cousin, Pam, was trying to do with her son. Yet Jackie never contacted me, even after I turned twenty-one. Not wanting to believe that she didn't care, I considered her death the only acceptable excuse.

The time came for the December meeting of the Adoption Identity Movement and I drove to the suburban library where they met. There were about fifteen people present, mostly women. Roughly two-thirds were adoptees and one-third were birth mothers. A few people already had completed their searches and shared heart-warming reunion stories.

I took notes and picked up various tips. For example, when visiting county offices to search for birth, marriage, or death records, you should never mention adoption. If you say you're doing genealogy research, the clerks will be much more cooperative.

Another tip: when you're writing to government offices for information, enclose a five-dollar money order for photocopies. This makes it more difficult for the clerks to ignore your request. They have to copy something to justify keeping the money. Or they have to send it back to you.

For me, the most fascinating part of the meeting was when each person described her situation and the status of her search. My turn came and I shared what I knew. When I mentioned my birth mother's possible death in an accident, several people exchanged knowing looks. When I asked what that was all about, the group's leader explained.

"The number one story children hear from adoptive parents is that one or both birth parents died in a traffic accident. A logical explanation, it is designed to close the discussion. But it usually isn't true."

I thought about that remark all the way home. Had my father told the truth when he said Jackie died in an accident? I didn't think he would lie under almost deathbed circumstances. But his stroke-damaged memory could have confused a thirty-year-old lie with the truth.

Then a more troubling possibility occurred to me. Perhaps someone lied to my father way back then. If my grandmother was paranoid enough to burn letters about my adoption, maybe she and my mother spread a false story about Jackie's death to stop anyone from trying to contact her.

The fact that "death in a traffic accident" was a widely used lie gave me a glimmer of hope that Jackie was alive. Maybe she did go on to become a college professor.

I didn't know what to think. Should I believe the people who were part of a lifelong cover-up who say she died? Or should I believe the anonymous source of a second-hand rumor who says she lived?

My head told me that Jackie was most likely dead. But my heart told me I had to look into the doctor-nurse scenario before I could rule it out.

I called Pat's cousin, Pam, in California and filled her in on my progress. Since I was born in Lansing, she suggested I contact a Lansing search group. She gave me the name and phone number of a woman named Jeanette from Adoptees Search for Knowledge (ASK).

When I reached Jeanette by phone, I learned that she had given up a baby for adoption and was still searching for her son. In the process, she met and began to help other birth mothers and adoptees reunite. Even after completing their searches, many of them viewed this as a noble cause and stuck around to help others.

Having seen the same attitude at the AIM meeting in Grand Rapids, I began to understand that adoption search was a national phenomenon with an army of foot soldiers anxious to help.

Jeanette proudly told me her group had completed over three hundred adoption searches. Only three times had the birth mother refused contact.

That was supposed to reassure me. But it raised an issue I had not even considered. What if I found Jackie alive and she wanted nothing to do with me? Or what if I found my brother and he rejected me?

I tried to put myself in the position of my birth mother. Having a child out of wedlock was considered far more shameful in the 1940s than it is today. Girls and their families went to extraordinary lengths to hide the pregnancy. Most birth families were as secretive on their end as my mother and grandmother were on my end. If the girls later married and had children, many would continue to hide that earlier "mistake" from their new families.

Jeanette told me that ASK met monthly at St. Lawrence Hospital in Lansing. I promised to attend the next meeting and marked the date on my calendar. Since I was born in that hospital, I found it ironic that my search was taking me back there.

On the day of the meeting, I took a half-day vacation and drove to East Lansing. I wanted some research time at the university library before the ASK meeting. December of 1981 had arrived and winter travel could be dicey. But the sun was shining and I felt invigorated by last month's decision to begin my search.

Michigan State University has one of the most beautiful campuses in the nation. Having spent four years there as an undergraduate and nearly two years getting my MBA, I knew the campus well. I took the East Lansing exit from the I-496 expressway and came in from the west on Kalamazoo Avenue.

I passed University Village, the married housing complex where Pat, Jenny, and I lived during grad school. The apartments were tiny and home to the occasional cockroach. But I remembered our life there with fondness. MSU was a great place to be. The building where we lived backed up to Kalamazoo Avenue and I could still pick out the bedroom windows of our old apartment.

The MSU Library is a huge, modern building wedged in among the ivy-covered buildings that mark the older, north side of campus. With classes in session, I knew there was a proverbial snowball's chance of finding a parking spot anywhere close. So I parked in the big visitor lot by Spartan Stadium and took the footbridge over the Red Cedar River to the back door of the library.

My research began with the faculty and staff directories from the 1960s. This was supposedly the era when my birth mother taught there. I wrote down the name of every woman professor or grad assistant with the first name of Jackie or Jacqueline.

Then I checked the MSU catalog from the 1945/'46 school year. I found that MSU had offered a major in Home Economics and Nursing in cooperation with the Sparrow Hospital School of Nursing. Sparrow was Lansing's other major hospital.

I went through the commencement listings for the 1940s to see who graduated with that degree. I found and recorded the few names that began with Jackie or Jacqueline. Then I looked up the women's photos in the corresponding college yearbooks and noted which ones had dark hair. As I looked at each photo, I wondered if I was seeing the face of my birth mother.

Next, I compared the names from the 1940s nursing school with the 1960s faculty names. There were no matches. This did not, however, prove the story was false. There may have been another nursing college in the area. Plus, the nursing students were most likely single and listed under their maiden names. Many of the women working for the university twenty years later would be married with new surnames.

I had hoped that something obvious would jump out at me—but nothing did. Checking my watch, I could hardly wait for my first meeting with Adoptees Search for Knowledge.

7

BREAKTHROUGH

After leaving the library, I grabbed a bite to eat in East Lansing and crossed the city limits into Lansing, arriving early at St. Lawrence Hospital. I found the ASK meeting and met Jeanette. The woman glowed with energy and enthusiasm. It was easy to see that adoption search was her passion.

Like the AIM group in Grand Rapids, almost everyone was female. It seemed reasonable that more birth mothers would be searching than birth fathers. Mothers had a lengthier and far more personal bond with a child they carried in their bodies for nine months. And some men might not know they had fathered a child.

Yet even the adoptees in the room were mostly women. I wondered how rare it was for a man to be searching. Men keep hearing that we are more shallow and less in touch with our feelings. That may explain why I did nothing until two women ganged up on me.

Like the AIM meeting I attended earlier, each person got a chance to tell her story and give a progress report. Others would chime in with questions and suggestions. It was a more productive use of brainstorming than anything I had seen in business. The difference, I think, was the genuine passion these people had for bringing about successful adoption reunions.

My story started a flutter of comments. Since many of those present were from the Lansing area, they searched their memories for doctors who looked like me. A few names came up as possibilities. One person thought I looked similar to a certain anesthesiologist and I wrote down his name. But nobody proclaimed an obvious match.

In the era of my birth, most doctors practicing in Michigan came from the in-state medical schools. Back then, that meant the University of Michigan or Wayne State University. Someone suggested I check the old yearbooks at those schools and browse the photos for men who looked like me.

I asked if there was any way to access the hospital records for my birth date to find my mother's full name on a patient listing. A woman who had worked at the hospital gave me the bad news. St. Lawrence Hospital routinely destroyed records more than twenty-five years old. Even the microfilm was gone.

The discussion then turned to locating Carol Woods, the daughter of the deceased couple that Dad said was connected to Jackie. She was the missing link to my birth family.

Since the Woods family had lived on the west side of Lansing, Carol went to Sexton High School. A year ahead of me, she would have been in the Class of 1963. A graduate of that high school said she would try to contact the class officers from Carol's class. Someone had to have an alumni mailing list for class reunions.

Another suggestion was to check the Polk's City Directories to confirm the address of the Woods home and track the family through the years. After the parents disappear from the alphabetical listings, I should use the section organized by street listings to find the next owner at that address. If Carol inherited the house, it might show her married name.

As I drove home that night, I realized that this last suggestion was brilliant. I was quite familiar with city directories. When I was still a toddler, Mom retired from the beauty shop business to be a full-time homemaker. But when I was in junior high, she took a temporary job gathering data for the Ionia City Directory. She would go door to door and interview people about their families and jobs.

In addition to paying her wages, the company sent her a copy of the new directory. I remember browsing the book, amazed at how it allowed you to snoop into people's lives.

Mom used her city directory experience to get a job as a census taker for the 1960 US Census. After that, she took a full-time job at Johnson's Drugs in Ionia. Her cosmetology background qualified her to advise people on cosmetics.

She also discovered a knack for picking products that would sell and she liked working with customers. The owner/pharmacist soon made her the manager of the entire store beyond the pharmacy, a job Mom held until she retired.

When I arrived home from the ASK meeting, I filled Pat in on what I learned. I vowed to follow up on the city directory tip and find Carol Woods.

———◆———

The following Saturday, I headed back to East Lansing, intent on checking the city directories at the university library. On the way there, I decided to detour through Lansing and cruise the street where the Woods family had lived. With luck, Carol might still be there. Or maybe the home's current owner would know where she went.

I remembered the street was behind the Oldsmobile Forge plant where Dad and Wayne both worked. To my amazement, it was gone. Not just the house; the street was gone. In fact, the whole neighborhood had vanished. As far as I could figure out, it had disappeared under an expanded factory parking lot.

When I found the old city directories in the library, I had a sudden idea. What if Jackie had been living with my parents when the survey taker stopped by in 1946? That person may have included her name as a boarder. Unfortunately, I soon discovered that World War II had interrupted the directory publishing business from 1941 to 1946, at least in Lansing.

Returning to my original task, I found the Woods family in the 1958 directory. The residence was 220 N. Alger Street. They listed Wayne's employment as tool and die at Oldsmobile.

I moved forward in time. In 1964, about the last time I had seen them, Wayne and Mildred were still in the alphabetical listings at the same address. The next directory was for the year 1967. The parents were gone. But I found a listing for Carol Woods with the same address. She had indeed inherited the house.

The next directory was the 1970 edition. I needed Carol to be there still and married. For that matter, I needed the house to be there still. I had no idea what year the wrecking ball arrived.

There was no Woods among the resident listings. Anxiously, I turned to the street listing section and found 220 N. Alger. Their old house was still standing in 1970. The owners were a Carl and a Carol with an unfamiliar last name.

That had to be it! Carol Woods married a man named Carl and I now knew her married name. I found a current Lansing telephone directory and said a silent prayer that they were still in the area. Sure enough, I found the address and phone number.

Since it was Saturday afternoon, I reasoned that I might be able to catch her at home. It was time for Carol to get a surprise visitor from her distant past.

About thirty minutes later, I parked on the street in front of Carol's home. It was only a few miles west of her old neighborhood and I had no trouble finding it.

I remained in the car, a little nervous about going to the door. How would Carol react to my showing up unannounced after nearly twenty years? Would she know anything at all about my adoption? And if she did, would she be willing to provide the information necessary to connect me to my mother and brother?

As I walked to the front door, I pumped up my courage and rang the bell. Fortunately, Carol was home and promptly answered the door. She looked like a slightly older version of the young girl I remembered. I knew right away that she recognized me, too, as a knowing smile appeared on her face. She spoke my name and invited me in.

Carl was out, so I did not get to meet him. Carol and I sat down in her living room and chatted for awhile, catching each other up on the spouses and children we had acquired since last seeing each other. Before I could get to the purpose of my visit, Carol beat me to it.

"You didn't drop by after all these years just to make small talk," she said. "You're here for a reason and I think I know what it is."

8

CAROL

I had found Carol and it seemed clear that she did know something about my adoption. Getting excited, I summarized my situation. I began with the 1964 revelation in the doctor's office and concluded with Dad's 1978 talc about Carol's parents, Wayne and Mickey, knowing my birth mother.

"I always knew you were adopted," volunteered Carol. "But it was a huge secret and my parents warned me never to tell you."

"Now that the secret is out," I asked, "what details do you know? How was my birth mother connected to your family?"

Carol paused for a moment to collect her thoughts. And then she told me. Her mother, Mickey, had an uncle in the Detroit area named Bill French, who had a wife, Marie, and three daughters. Bill worked at the Kelvinator plant and began having an affair with a divorced coworker named Marion.

Bill would move in with Marion for months and then go back to his wife for awhile. The cycle repeated many times over a span of six years or so. In the end, Marie filed for divorce and Bill eventually married Marion in about 1951.

During one of the times that Bill and Marion were living together, Marion's daughter, Jackie, got pregnant and needed to find a home for her baby. Bill remembered that his Lansing niece, Mickey, wanted to adopt a child.

So in December 1945, Mickey received a call from her Uncle Bill asking if she and Wayne would adopt this baby. Bill did not know that Mickey and Wayne had just adopted Carol, who was born that November.

"You almost became my brother," laughed Carol. "But my parents could not imagine having two babies only six months apart in age. Plus, my adoption had been anonymous and that was the way they wanted it. Adopting Marion's grandchild would have been awkward."

Carol went on to explain that her parents recommended a good alternative. Wayne had a friend at Oldsmobile who wanted to adopt a baby. That, of course, was Harold Hill, the man I knew as my father.

At last, one piece of my story fell into place. I knew exactly how Jackie ended up in a Lansing apartment with my adoptive parents. I could now connect the dots.

Carol did not know if Jackie was dead or alive. Yet she was sure she could find out. Marion had died in 1969 and Bill was in a nursing home. But Bill's ex-wife, Marie, and their daughters were still alive and would know more.

Then Carol smiled as she remembered an incident from our high school years.

"Do you remember a time when you and your parents dropped in to see us and then your mother made some excuse to leave right away?"

I told her I did not remember it and Carol continued her story.

In about 1963, Kelvinator closed the Detroit plant where Bill and Marion worked. Since both were without jobs, they came to Lansing and moved in with Bill's sister, Fannie.

"Wait a minute," I said. "Wasn't Fannie your grandmother, the one who lived in the house next to yours?"

"That's right," chuckled Carol. "When you and your parents showed up that day, your biological grandmother, Marion, was living next door.

She could have dropped in at any minute and would have been thrilled to see you."

Carol continued, "My mother took your mother aside to warn her. Then Thelma yanked you and your father out of here like the house was on fire. It was so funny."

We shared a good laugh about that story. Now I understood why I had not seen the Woods family after high school. Whatever relationship my parents continued to have with Carol's parents, they never included me.

Then I changed the subject.

"I didn't know you were adopted. Have you ever thought about searching for your birth mother?"

She replied that she had always known and was not especially curious about her biological family. She understood that some adoptees felt a need to search, but she never did. We agreed that it should be an individual decision. In any case, Carol was quite willing to help me with my search.

I told Carol about the rumor that my mother was a nurse and my father a Lansing doctor. She had never heard any such thing. The only nurse involved in my story was Carol's mother. Mickey had worked at St. Lawrence Hospital until Carol was born.

Rumors often have a kernel of truth that distorts as more people retell the story. I wondered if my parents finding my birth mother *through* a nurse morphed into my birth mother *being* a nurse. Maybe. But I still couldn't imagine where the part about my father being a doctor came from.

Carol promised to call Bill's ex-wife, Marie, for details and report back to me. I got back in my car and drove home feeling pretty good that the pieces were falling into place.

The next day was Sunday and I hung around home all day, not wanting to miss Carol's call. In late afternoon, the phone rang at last and I heard Carol's voice. She had reached Marie, who then called two of her daughters, Barb and Lorraine. They compared their recollections and then Barb called Carol with a summary. Carol took notes so she could relay the facts to me.

My mother's maiden name was Jackie Hartzell. The Hartzell name came from Marion's first husband, whom they never knew. The marriage produced three daughters: Marilyn, Jackie, and Joyce. Marion's second husband was Johnny Ratkewicz, but that marriage didn't last long.

Jackie left high school early to get married. Her husband was Leonard Bojanzyk. So her legal married name was Jacqueline Bojanzyk. She and Leonard did have a son, but their marriage ended in divorce. When Jackie found herself pregnant again in 1945, she chose to put me up for adoption.

When I heard this, I wondered if Leonard might be my father, even though they had split up. If so, her first son and I would be full brothers. If there was a new man involved, we would be half brothers.

As I took all this down, my mind raced ahead.

"Was Jackie killed in an auto accident?"

I held my breath as Carol provided the answer.

"Yes, Jackie and her younger sister, Joyce, both died in the accident. Barb and her family can't agree on the timing, but it would have been just a year or two after you were born."

Even though I had expected this news, I still felt a little pang of sorrow to learn that Jackie had died so young. I also felt guilty for even thinking that Mom and my grandmother might have made up a story about Jackie's death. Thankfully, I had never shared that crazy theory with anyone.

At least I did not have to waste any more time pursuing the doctor-nurse scenario. I now knew it was false. The best news of all was that I now knew my brother's surname. He would be a Bojanzyk and, with luck, might still be living in the Detroit area. The universe of possibilities had shrunk dramatically.

"What about Jackie's older sister, Marilyn," I asked. "Does anyone know what happened to her?"

"As far as they know," Carol replied, "Marilyn is still alive and somewhere in the Detroit area. But no one can remember her married name. So that is not much to go on."

I then asked Carol if anyone knew the identity of my biological father.

"This is where it gets awkward," replied Carol. "There was a rumor at the time that your father was a relative of Marie's. That man is still alive and married. They won't tell me his name."

"Do you have any idea who they might be referring to?" I asked. Carol did not. But she had a bunch of old family photos tucked away somewhere in her house. There would be pictures from family reunions and other events. She promised to search for those pictures, go through them with a fresh eye, and check for men who looked like me.

Even though Carol wasn't curious about her own birth parents, my mystery had captivated her. She had even called the Lansing nursing home where her Great Uncle, Bill French, resided. They told her that he had good days and bad days. If I could catch him on a good day, perhaps he might remember something helpful.

A few days after that call from Carol, I decided it was time for me to make another trip to Lansing.

It was still December and I burned another half day of vacation. My first stop was Bill's nursing home. When I said I was there to visit Bill French, someone directed me to a man in a wheelchair, sitting idly in the hallway. He was thin and frail looking.

Kneeling by his chair, I asked if he was Bill. He nodded. I had been hoping he might recall something about his wife Marion's daughters. But his mind was so far gone that he didn't even remember Marion.

I had not known this man. Yet I couldn't help feeling sorry for him. It had to be tough when your mind failed years before your body did.

From there I went to the state library on Michigan Avenue, where they had the Detroit newspapers on microfilm. I started with my birth date and reviewed the papers going forward for nearly a year.

I didn't know if Jackie's accident would be front-page news or not. So I scanned the most likely sections of each daily issue. It was tedious work. After several hours, I gave up and went home.

Even though this trip had been a bust, I reflected on the drive back to Grand Rapids that I had made a lot of progress in less than thirty days. I now knew the identity of my birth mother and the last name of my brother. And with Carol's help, we might be able to figure out which of Marie's relatives was the man suspected of being my father.

9

ETHNIC SOUP

Dad had described Jackie as Irish, but her maiden name, Hartzell, didn't sound Irish to me. I had never heard the name and could not associate it with any particular country.

Her married name, Bojanzyk, was also unfamiliar to me. It sounded like it might be Polish, but I couldn't be sure. In any case, it was the name of my brother's father, who was unlikely to be my father.

Growing up with an unknown ethnic background is something that bothers many adoptees. In my case, I grew up not even knowing about my adoption.

Moreover, I could only describe my adoptive family as ethnically neutral. When I first realized that my genes came from an unknown family, I had no sense of a missing ethnicity. My parents had already infused me with an identity that was purely American.

I remember a grade school assignment where my teacher asked each student to share something about his or her family's ethnic background. I had to go home and ask what we were. I didn't have a clue.

Mom told me that Dad's father was English and his mother was German. As for her ancestors, Mom had heard they were Welsh and Irish with a touch of American Indian. But nobody could identify the specific Indian ancestor or the tribe.

I questioned Dad that weekend and he just joked that I was a Heinz. When I asked what that meant, he said "57 varieties."

In truth, the genealogy bug had never bitten my family. Ancestors prior to my great-grandparents were nameless. We had no family Bible handed down with carefully recorded births and marriages. While many families could trace their ancestry to "the old country," my adoptive family's tree couldn't even get out of Michigan.

My wife, Pat, had a more distinct ethnic background. While her mother's side was another mixed bag of Western European ancestries, her father had been 100 percent Croatian. His parents had immigrated separately to the United States in the early 1900s.

They met in the Croatian community of East Chicago, where Pat's grandfather worked in a steel mill. Ultimately, they saved enough money to fulfill an immigrant's dream and buy a small farm. This one happened to be in Michigan.

Pat grew up with a lot of Slavic neighbors, including Czechs, Slovaks, and Poles. Those in her grandparents' generation, who spoke little English, were able to communicate through similar native tongues.

In the twentieth century, Croatia had been part of Austria and then part of Yugoslavia. Outside of certain cities with large Croatian communities, Pat's ethnic group was virtually unknown in Middle America.

Whenever Pat said she was Croatian, most people responded with blank stares. So my mother started introducing Pat as her "Polack daughter-in-law." Since Polack jokes were making the rounds, Mom thought this was hugely funny. Although Pat made it clear she did not appreciate the humor, we could not stop my mother from saying it.

The Monday after I met with Carol, I received a letter from the Ingham County Probate Court with my non-identifying information. They said my mother was five feet three inches tall and weighed 110 pounds with brown hair. My father was five feet eight inches tall, weighed 155 pounds, and had dark blond hair.

Jackie's description was consistent with what I had heard about her. But the description of my birth father was a shock. According to this, he was an inch shorter than my adoptive father! Where on earth did my height come from? I had always visualized my mystery father as a tall man.

There was a section on educational level, which said my mother had finished the eleventh grade and my father, the twelfth. Her information was consistent with the fact that Jackie had quit school early to get married.

Under religion, they had my father as a Protestant while my mother's religion was "not indicated."

The status of termination could be voluntary or court-ordered. Mine was voluntary.

There was a section about age and sex of siblings at the time of my adoption. It said "Boy, 2½."

There it was in black and white: legal proof of what my father had told me and Carol's family had confirmed. I did have a brother! And now I knew the difference in our ages. He must have been born in the fall of 1943.

There was nothing to indicate the age of either parent. So I would not be able to use age to confirm a suspected father.

The medical information section had nothing on either parent. It did give my weight and length at birth with an update of those numbers at nine months. They also knew I was cutting teeth at ten months and allergic to acids, fruits, and tomatoes.

There must have been a social worker checking up on me. The report described me as "creeping and standing in a playpen at nine months and a very happy child."

Pat and I were standing at the kitchen table reading this letter together. Suddenly, Pat started to laugh so hard that she could hardly catch her breath. Wondering what would trigger such a response, I moved my eyes to the bottom of the page.

Under ethnicity of biological parents, I saw what Pat found so uproariously funny: my father was Polish.

When Pat was composed enough to speak, she said, "For thirteen years your mother has been calling me a Polack. Now this shows that her little boy is the real Polack in the family. I should call her right now and tell her the good news."

Pat would not make that call, of course, because Mom was still unaware that I knew about my adoption and was searching for my brother. Still, I noticed a satisfied smirk on Pat's face that lingered for days.

Personally, I never cared what my ethnic background turned out to be. I just thought it was nice to have one.

10

LIES

A couple days after the letter from the Ingham County Probate Court arrived, I received an envelope from the Michigan Department of Public Health.

I had been wondering how the bureaucrats in Lansing would respond to my request for a birth certificate. It was highly unlikely that they would provide my actual birth certificate with the names of my biological parents. The most likely response, I imagined, would be a certificate of adoption listing my adoptive parents. Or they might just give me some excuse that my birth certificate was lost or otherwise unavailable.

As hard as I thought, I could not imagine any other possibility. Then I opened the envelope and discovered a full-fledged birth certificate listing Harold and Thelma Hill as my biological parents.

Embossed with the official seal of the Michigan Department of Public Health, it included the signature of the state registrar who declared: "*I hereby certify that the above is a true and correct transcript of the record of birth on file in the Michigan Department of Public Health.*"

This was an outright lie. Two days earlier I had received a letter from another government entity, the Ingham County Probate Court, which proved it was a lie.

In an instant, I realized that the vast conspiracy to cover up my adoption had even included the state of Michigan. I was speechless and outraged at the same time.

Adoptees routinely complain about the injustice of not letting adults see their own birth records. But somehow, this seemed much worse. In my opinion, the state had crossed the line from secrecy into outright fraud.

I wasn't a genealogist then. But I knew that people building their family trees depended on the government's vital records of birth, marriage, and death. Hundreds of years from now people would be digging through these records expecting them to be the gospel truth. How could the state of Michigan falsify the history of its citizens?

With all this new information and a sense of moral outrage, I got on the phone and called Jeanette, the founder of Adoptees Search for Knowledge, in Lansing. When I started spouting off about the false birth certificate, she stopped me.

"I could have told you that's what you would get. It happens all the time."

Calming down, I relayed my non-identifying information. I also filled her in on the details I received through Carol, including my birth mother's name, Jackie Hartzell, and the name of her husband, Leonard Bojanzyk.

Jeanette got out the Detroit area telephone directory she kept in her personal research library and looked for his name. There were seven listings for Bojanzyk, but Leonard was not among them.

"I'll bet that one of these names is your brother," she said. "I know how to make these inquiries without scaring people off. Would you like me to locate your brother?"

Knowing I would be too nervous to make those calls myself, I told her to go ahead.

Like a sergeant in the adoption search army, Jeanette then proceeded to give me my marching orders. She had two things she wanted me to work on while she was probing for my brother. I agreed to do both.

First, she wanted me to write again for my birth certificate. I was to give them the same city and date of birth. But this time, I should sign my name as Richard Bojanzyk. Since Jackie had been a Bojanzyk by marriage, my real birth certificate was probably in that name. If my birth certificate had a first name other than Richard, this might not work. But it was worth a try.

Second, she wanted me to get phone numbers from Carol for Barb and Lorraine, the daughters of Bill French who had provided the details about Jackie. I should call them myself and see what else they remembered. Moreover, I should share the non-identifying information on my birth father and ask if it matched the man rumored to be my father.

Carol only had the number for Barb, the one who had called her. I called Barb and she gave me Lorraine's number. After talking with each of them, I did acquire some additional information.

Barb and Lorraine were teenagers when their father, Bill, began his affair with Jackie's mother, Marion. They lived outside Detroit in Livonia Township and went to Plymouth High School. Lorraine, the older one, was the same age as Jackie's younger sister, Joyce, and rode the school bus with her.

The Hartzell girls had moved into the area and lived in a small rental house on Plymouth Road near Stark Street.

At the time Jackie and Joyce died, their older sister, Marilyn, was already married and had a family. For the younger girls, death occurred when a Jeep they were riding in rolled over after leaving Cavalcade Inn, a bar owned by the driver. It had been a popular spot on Northville Road near Phoenix Lake.

I pushed a little to see if Barb or Lorraine might tell me the name of my suspected father. No dice. So I shared the non-identifying data the court had provided about my birth father. Other than being a Protestant, they both said nothing else matched. The man they were protecting could not be the man described in my file.

11

ELEANOR

Once she got going, it did not take Jeanette long to identify my brother. It was still December 1981 and she called me on a Monday night with a progress report.

Looking at the seven Bojanzyks in the Detroit phone directory, she had started with Eugene. His wife answered and confirmed that Leonard was a cousin. Married several times, Leonard now lived in California. He did have two brothers in the Detroit area: Joseph and Richard.

Joseph's number was unlisted, so Jeanette called Richard. He didn't know where in California Leonard lived and didn't care, calling him a "pain in the ass." He didn't have anything good to say about Joseph, either.

Continuing the conversation, Jeanette learned that the men's mother had died three years earlier and the entire family had been embroiled in a battle over her estate. They had settled it the previous Friday, so the wounds were still fresh.

Richard mentioned that Leonard had a son. Raised by his grandparents, this nephew of Richard's was more like a kid brother. His name was Michael.

As Jeanette told me this, I paused to reflect on the name I finally heard for the first time at age thirty-five: Michael Bojanzyk. This was my brother.

When Jeanette told Richard about me and the purpose of her call, he did not believe her. He had never even heard that Leonard and Jackie had been divorced. And he certainly did not believe that Jackie had another son.

Richard admitted that he was only twelve years old when his older brother's wife died and he could have been shielded from such adult matters. But if Jackie had another son, he reasoned, someone would surely have mentioned it when he was older. Jeanette left her name and phone number with Richard and then called me.

Although Michael's number was in the phone book, Jeanette insisted that we not contact him directly until we found someone in the family to confirm my story. Fortunately, that did not take long.

Two nights later, I was getting ready for bed when the phone rang. It was Jeanette again and she was excited. After thinking about her peculiar call, Richard contacted a previously unmentioned sister.

That sister, Eleanor, knew about Jackie's second baby.

After filling Richard in on the story that he had been too young to hear, Eleanor called Jeanette. She had always wondered what happened to Jackie's second child. Quite excited, she wanted me to call her right away. It didn't matter how late it was. Eleanor would wait up for my call.

With my own excitement growing, I finished my conversation with Jeanette and dialed Eleanor's number. She answered right away and we talked for nearly an hour.

Jackie had been Eleanor's best friend in high school and someone she fondly remembered as "a beautiful person." Eleanor described Jackie as short with a small nose, freckles, and blue eyes.

The two of them were classmates at Plymouth High School until Jackie quit school at age sixteen to marry Eleanor's brother, Leonard. Jackie and Leonard's son, Michael, was born in October 1943 when Jackie was seventeen.

"Leonard was a lousy brother and a worse husband," Eleanor exclaimed. "He treated Jackie badly and I helped her leave him in December 1944."

Jackie and Michael moved in with her mother, Marion, and Jackie found a job. Her mother worked a different schedule so they had a plan for the baby's care. But Marion proved to be an unreliable sitter.

"Marion liked her drinks," Eleanor explained.

With no other options, Jackie decided to entrust her baby to Mrs. Bojanzyk, Leonard's mother. It was to be a temporary arrangement until Jackie could save enough money to support her son.

I told Eleanor how Marion's connection to Bill French had led to my adoption in Lansing. Eleanor had gone to school with Lorraine French and knew about Marion's long-running affair with Bill.

Eleanor had learned about me when a letter came to the Bojanzyk home notifying Leonard that Jackie had given birth and put the baby up for adoption. Since Jackie got pregnant before the divorce was final, Leonard was legally my father and the court had to notify him of the adoption.

Eleanor was certain, however, that Leonard was not my biological father. Once Jackie left him, he moved to the other side of town and they had nothing to do with each other. So Michael and I were surely half brothers.

After dropping Michael off at the Bojanzyk home, Jackie began to run around with a crowd from Northville, a town just north of Plymouth. Eleanor had heard that Jackie was involved with the guy who owned the bar where she worked.

Remembering what Barb and Lorraine had told me about the fatal Jeep accident, I questioned Eleanor.

"Was that the guy from Cavalcade Inn?"

"Yes, I think so," she said. "I can't remember the guy's name. But I do remember the owner of Cavalcade Inn had been driving under the influence of alcohol and was responsible for Jackie's death."

"Years later," she continued, "The guy did it again and killed two more people in another accident."

I had a distressing thought. What if my biological father was the man who caused my birth mother's death and then went on to kill more people? I prayed that my father was someone else. Anyone else.

Eleanor went on to say that the sudden death of Jackie and Joyce had been big news. Plymouth and Northville were small towns and both girls were popular and well liked. Plus, both were young parents. In Joyce's case, she left behind a little girl.

When asked, Eleanor placed the date of the accident as June 1947. I did the math. Jackie died just thirteen months after I was born. She was only twenty-one.

Eleanor vividly remembered the funeral at the Schrader Funeral Home in Plymouth.

"The girls are buried in Grand Lawn Cemetery near Redford," she continued.

We then turned our discussion to Michael—or Mike, as most people called him now. Mike was divorced and his nine-year-old daughter lived with his ex-wife.

Eleanor promised to call Mike the next day and have him call me. With all this news to absorb and the anticipation of speaking to my brother, I had a hard time sleeping that night.

12

MICHAEL

The next evening I received the call I had been looking forward to ever since I started my search.

"This is Mike Bojanzyk," the caller said. "I understand we may be brothers."

Mike's attitude was friendly enough. But I could tell he was shell-shocked. He explained that his Uncle Richard called first and told him about me. Then he got a second call from his Aunt Eleanor.

Eleanor claimed she had told him about Jackie's second baby when his grandmother died three years earlier. But he did not remember the conversation. There had been a lot of wrangling over the grandmother's estate and that had weighed heavily on his mind for a long time.

Today's conversation with Eleanor had challenged much of what Mike thought was his personal history. He knew that he had come to live with his grandparents when he was about eighteen months old. But he had always assumed that was a direct result of his mother's sudden death.

Mike was stunned to learn that Jackie lived another two years after he arrived at his grandmother's home. When he told me that, I realized that my family wasn't the only one to keep secrets from its children.

In her call, Eleanor told Mike that she had taken him to see his mother once. But he could not remember it, of course. He was not yet four years old when Jackie died.

In addition to having no memories of his mother, Mike had few good memories of his father. Leonard remarried and had other children. For brief periods, Mike had moved in with his father and stepmother. But it never worked out well and Mike always ended up back with his grandmother.

In more recent years, Leonard had lived in California. He only called his son when he wanted something, usually to borrow money. The extended fight over the family estate had been the final blow to their strained relationship and Mike had written off his father completely.

I shared what I knew about Jackie coming to Lansing during her second pregnancy and living with my adoptive parents. I told him how I had grown up in Ionia, about two hours west of him. Then I explained how a doctor had revealed my adoption and how my father later told me I had a brother.

While I was excited enough to talk all night, I could tell that Mike needed time just to absorb the basic facts surrounding our relationship. I had known about him for almost four years. But he had only known about me for a few hours. We agreed to talk again soon and ended the call.

After hanging up with Mike, I immediately called his aunt, Eleanor. She told me she had been so excited from our conversation the night before that she had not gone to bed until 4 a.m.

Because of the letter the Probate Court had sent to her brother, Leonard, regarding my adoption, Eleanor had known about me most of my life. Her conversation with Jeanette had ended three decades of speculation.

A few years ago, she had even thought about trying to find me. But she had no idea how to get started. All she knew was that Jackie had given up a baby boy for adoption in Ingham County.

Eleanor remembered that Jackie had adored Leonard's little brother, Richard. She wondered if Jackie might have suggested the name to my adoptive parents. Since no one else in my adoptive family carried the name Richard, I thought she might be right.

Eleanor told me that Leonard had gone into the service while Jackie was pregnant with Mike, but he managed to get an early discharge.

Then, when Mike was still a baby, Leonard would disappear for two or three days at a time, sometimes leaving his wife and child in the house with no food. That was why, when Jackie decided to leave him, Eleanor had helped her move out.

According to Eleanor, Jackie changed once she was free of her abusive husband and Mike was safely tucked away at his grandmother's home.

In the two years between dropping Mike off with Eleanor's mother and her death in the accident, Jackie only tried to visit Mike once. On that occasion, she stopped by the Bojanzyk home with two other girls and three guys.

"All of them had obviously been drinking," Eleanor explained. "Because of that, my mother and I would not let Jackie come in to see Mike."

Eleanor assured me that Jackie would have been welcome otherwise. But she never came back.

I had wondered earlier if Jackie ever thought about finding me. After hearing this, I figured I knew the answer to that question.

We ended that call, but Eleanor called me back the following night. Mike had filled her in on his conversation with me. He was still struggling with all the unexpected news about our mother and me.

Since Mike was not close to his dad or his dad's other kids, he would welcome a good relationship with me. But having been hurt so many times by his family, he was afraid of being hurt again. Eleanor encouraged me to call Mike again on Saturday.

I did as she suggested and Mike and I had our second phone conversation. He seemed more relaxed this time and we filled each other in on the separate lives we had lived to this point.

Mike owned a home in a Detroit suburb. He had gone to college at Eastern Michigan University. Ever since graduation, he had been a physical education teacher in an elementary school.

His daughter would be ten in October. She lived in Ohio with his ex-wife, but she would be up to see him for Christmas. Mike had a girlfriend that he had been dating for five years. She was also divorced and her son lived with her.

Wondering if we had inherited any common maladies, Mike and I compared notes on medical conditions. Both of us were healthy, so there wasn't much to discuss. But we did find one interesting commonality. Each of us had undergone surgery for a deviated septum to solve sinus problems.

Mike and I then set a date to meet in person at Eleanor's house after the holidays. We exchanged addresses and promised to send pictures in the meantime. The timing was good, Mike said, because he had just gotten his annual photo package from the school where he worked.

I asked Mike if he had any pictures of himself as a child. Mike explained that all of his childhood photos were in his grandmother's home, now occupied by his Uncle Joseph. The fact that Joseph got the home was one of the sore points in the estate fight and no one in the family was speaking to him.

We said good-bye and got busy with our own families for the Christmas holidays. I sent Mike a Christmas card and enclosed a few photos of myself. Then I received a card from Mike.

Excitedly, I looked at the enclosed photo and was shocked to see a guy with curly brown hair. My hair is totally straight.

Anticipating my surprise, Mike had thoughtfully written the following note on the card:

"The hair is not naturally curly. I get a perm every three months."

Saturday, January 9, 1982, was the big day to meet Mike. Pat and I loaded up the kids into our Volvo station wagon and made the two-hour drive to the home of Mike's Aunt Eleanor in the Detroit suburbs.

People everywhere remember Michigan as the state shaped like a mitten. In reality, this Great Lakes state is more like three separate states that don't have much to do with each other.

First, there is southeast Michigan, which radiates out to some reasonable commuting distance from Detroit. Secondly, there is the rest of the Lower Peninsula, including the Grand Rapids area where I live and the state capital of Lansing, where I was born.

Lastly, there is the Upper Peninsula, the land above the mitten known for six-foot snow drifts and people who proudly call themselves Yoopers.

Michiganders from outside the Detroit area have little reason to go there. Even though fifteen years had passed since Detroit's infamous 1967 riot, many people in 1982 were still afraid of our biggest city.

Fortunately, I wasn't one of them. I had visited Detroit a few times on business. Plus, Pat had an aunt and uncle who lived just outside the city. So we knew the Detroit suburbs could be just as nice and safe as the suburbs of Grand Rapids.

Jenny was eight and seemed to understand that we were going to meet a brother I had never seen. The twins, now three, just accepted the trip as another family outing. As usual, they occupied the rear-facing third seat of our station wagon and waved at the cars behind us.

When we arrived at Eleanor's house, Mike was not yet there. Eleanor invited us in and introduced us to her husband. As it turned out, he kept our kids entertained for much of the day so the rest of us could get to know each other.

Even though Eleanor was Mike's aunt, not mine, she was absolutely thrilled to meet me in person. She had known for thirty-five years that her deceased friend, Jackie, had another child out there somewhere. And she was obviously proud of her role in reuniting Jackie's two children.

Mike arrived a little while later. Our first meeting was nothing like the adoption reunions captured for television. Those people always seem to be a mother and daughter or two sisters. They always hug each other immediately and the tears start to flow.

As grown men, Mike and I simply shook hands.

Our manly reserve did not change the fact that this was a huge deal for me. Except for my children, this was the first time I ever laid eyes on a blood relative.

Mike looked just like his picture, curly hair and all. He was tall, only an inch shorter than I was. But other than that, I did not see much resemblance. Of course, even full brothers don't always look alike. And Mike and I only had one parent in common.

Fortunately, Eleanor had one photo of Mike as a young boy. His natural hair back then was just as straight as mine. Everyone agreed that we looked much more alike as children.

Mike brought his longtime girlfriend, an attractive blonde woman who we learned was an aerobics instructor. She was warm and friendly and Pat and I liked her right away.

Everyone wanted to hear my story. How and when did I learn I had a brother? Then, how did I discover it was Mike? After covering that icebreaker topic, Mike and I talked more about our current lives.

I learned that Mike's bachelor life revolved almost entirely around sports. Depending on the season, he was in leagues for golf, bowling, and softball. In addition to his men's leagues, he and his girlfriend were in some co-ed leagues. In the winter, they also went downhill skiing.

Mike was an avid fan of all the Detroit pro sports teams. Although he got his degree from Eastern Michigan University, the college whose teams he rooted for was the University of Michigan.

As a fan of Michigan State, I found Mike's preference for my school's archrival disheartening. But since he was my brother, I chose to overlook that single flaw in his character.

My sporting life paled in comparison. I used to play golf on rare occasions, but had given it up when life got too busy. Now with three small children, the closest I came to participating in a sport was playing tee-ball or soccer with my kids and their friends in the backyard.

Expecting our common genes to result in common interests, I was a little disappointed.

At the end of the day, Mike and I posed for pictures together. I could tell Mike was still a little reserved about me. But I was optimistic that we would grow closer as time went on and we got a chance to know each other better.

On the way home, Pat and I talked about the need to stay in touch with Mike and work on building a good relationship. We hoped he would visit us in the coming months.

That brought up a scary thought. My adoptive mother, with whom I had never discussed my adoption, had a habit of dropping in unannounced to see her grandchildren and us. What if she showed up sometime when Mike was there?

After thirty-five years, she still assumed my adoption was a secret. Reluctantly, I realized it was time for me to open this subject. Besides revealing that I had known and kept quiet about my adoption for the past seventeen years, I would have to tell her that I had now found my brother.

13

CONFESSION

I have never enjoyed confrontations, verbal or otherwise. And, frankly, I was terrified of confessing to my adoptive mother that I was only pretending to be ignorant of my adoption and, furthermore, I had actually searched for and found my brother.

Would she cry? Would she get mad? Would she walk out in a huff? Having seen all those reactions from her over much smaller issues, I decided to write a letter.

Some would say this was a coward's way out. I like to think of it as an act of courtesy…giving her a chance to absorb the entire message and reflect on it privately before we talked.

I saved the messy draft of my letter. So I can quote the key parts of it here:

Dear Mom,

I have some good news that I want to share with you. I hope you will see it as good news, too. But it deals with a subject that you and I have avoided discussing for thirty-five years: my adoption.

When I was growing up, you and Dad never told me I was adopted. Or if you did, I wasn't paying attention and can't remember it. When I was eighteen, Dr. Campbell casually mentioned my adoption during an office visit just before I started college.

Although many people today are more open about this subject, I understand that things were different when I was born. So your secrecy is certainly understandable. And I don't believe that the secrecy or my finding out about it later caused me any harm.

Knowing about my adoption has never made me feel any differently about you. While almost anyone can conceive a child, it takes real love and commitment to raise one.

I wanted to talk to you about this for many years. But you and Dad seemed content with the ongoing secrecy. You never brought it up and I never found the nerve to speak first.

Then, during one of my lunchtime visits with Dad during his year at Kent Community Hospital, he suddenly mentioned the subject. He told me that Wayne and Mickey Woods put my birth mother, Jackie, in touch with you. He also explained how Jackie lived with you for awhile, and how you brought me home from the hospital right after I was born.

Dad then told me about Jackie's death in an accident. And he also told me that Jackie had an older son who would be my half brother. In fact, he kept urging me to find my brother. But Wayne and Mickey were already gone. And I knew you were going through a rough time, so I chose not to ask you for information.

Mom, I know how special your brother and sister were to you. So you can understand how I might want to find the brother I never knew. To make a long story short, I have recently found him. We've talked on the phone, exchanged pictures, and this past Saturday I finally met him.

His name is Mike Bojanzyk. Some non-identifying information I got from the Probate Court says my birth father was also Polish. So please take it easy on the Polack jokes!

I've learned a great deal about my background and the people involved. It has been fascinating. Plus, knowing the truth about myself makes me feel more complete. I'm mature enough to handle it now and I'm sure you are, too.

Knowing the situation with my birth mother, I feel even more thankful that you and Dad got to raise me. I will always consider you my real parents.

My brother, Mike, and I will be getting together again from time to time. Perhaps you will meet him someday. I'm sure you'll like him.

In the meantime, I hope we can discuss this subject freely. Dad certainly felt relieved to get this subject out into the open and I'm praying that you will, too.

I signed the letter with "love" and added a P.S. We were going to see her on Sunday. So I let her know she was welcome to call me at home or at work should she prefer to talk before then.

A couple evenings later, the phone rang at home. It was Mom and she was ready to talk.

Mom said she had received the letter and was not upset. She explained that she and Dad had told me about my adoption when I was quite young. They even read to me from a book called "The Chosen Baby."

But a neighbor treated me as an outcast and would not let her children play with "the little bastard." So they decided to shut up about my adoption to prevent discrimination.

What a moron, I thought. Did that neighbor think her kids would catch something from me—cooties, perhaps? Was adoption itself some low-class form of parenthood?

I was beginning to grasp the different thinking that prevailed in the 1940s.

Now I could guess why I had gone all though elementary and high school without ever encountering an openly adopted child. Their families were also sidestepping prejudice by not talking about it.

Mom's story made sense to me. I did not remember anything from my toddler years. So I could not have remembered any stories about adoption. Plus, psychologists say that children cannot grasp the concept of adoption until they are at least five years old.

By the time I was five, my aunts and my parents' women friends had all stopped bearing children. So I never saw anything in my early childhood years to make me wonder about the origins of children. I can't even remember seeing a pregnant woman until I was probably ten years old.

By then, the wall of secrecy surrounding my adoption had been in place for years.

Now that Mom had explained the secrecy, I moved to the question I was dying to ask.

"Did Jackie ever say anything to you about the identity of my biological father?"

Mom replied that Jackie had not told them anything about him. She thought she heard somewhere that he had been in the army.

I'm sure I smiled into the phone. Since my conception occurred right at the end of World War II, that clue, even if true, could only narrow my search to a few million men.

I next asked her if Jackie's ex-husband, Leonard, could have been my father. She was certain it was not him.

I told her I had heard a rumor that it might be someone in Mickey's family. She said Mickey had checked out that rumor and found it to be false.

Unable to think of anything better to say, I mentioned the other rumor about my father being a doctor. She said that Jackie would not have run in that kind of crowd.

Mom then made her opinion of Jackie quite clear.

"She was a tramp. She couldn't wait to get rid of you and get back to her parties."

I didn't like hearing that, but I respected Mom's right to have an opinion. I wondered if her harsh assessment was partly due to jealousy. She had yearned to bear a child but could not. Yet this young, fertile woman had done it twice by the time she was twenty.

Mom then discouraged me from getting involved with Jackie's family, calling them a bad bunch. Yet the only one Mom could have known was my biological grandmother, Marion. Since other people had already positioned Marion as an alcoholic and a home wrecker, I didn't know what to say about that.

"One more question," I asked. "Where did my name Richard come from? I know it is not a name from our family. Did Jackie suggest it?"

"No," came her terse reply. "It was just a name your Dad and I liked."

If Jackie had suggested my name, Mom was not about to give her any credit. I thanked Mom for the call and we ended the conversation.

None of this was mentioned the following Sunday when Pat and I saw Mom in person. It was as though the letter had never been sent and the follow-up discussion had never happened.

One thing apparently did stick: from that day on, I never heard Mom joke about Polacks.

14

PAPER TRAILS

Having achieved my immediate goals, I could have stopped my search. After all, I had learned the identity of my birth mother, confirmed Dad's story of her death, and met my brother.

Diving into my search, I had neglected every other facet of my life. What's more, between my own phone calls and Jeanette's, I had incurred hundreds of dollars in long distance charges in just two months.

While the cost was high, I did not regret any of it. Unfortunately, I did not experience any sense of closure. I think this was partly because I could not meet my birth mother. In addition, my list of unanswered questions was getting longer instead of shorter.

What did Jackie look like? I knew she was short with blue eyes and dark hair. But no one I had met yet, not even Mike, had any pictures of her.

Who was my father? Could I be 100 percent certain that Mike's father was not my father, too? A short, light-haired Polish guy, Leonard matched the physical description in my non-identifying information.

Only the religion didn't match. The court said my father was a Protestant. The Bojanzyk family was Catholic.

Who was the rumored father that Carol's family was protecting? Had Mickey Woods actually confirmed that rumor was not true? Or was my adoptive mother just trying to keep me from searching further?

Had Jackie been dating the Cavalcade Inn owner who crashed the Jeep and killed her and her sister, Joyce?

Could I find Jackie's older sister, Marilyn, my biological aunt, or the daughter of Jackie's younger sister Joyce, who would be my cousin?

My initial search had proceeded like a car racing down the highway. Now it seemed reasonable to let up on the accelerator a little. But there was no way I was going to hit the brakes.

This was a crucial part of my personal history. I now felt compelled to learn all I could about my birth parents and their families.

As a father of three, I realized that I wasn't only searching for my own benefit. I wanted a complete family history to pass on to my children and grandchildren.

That was one reason I kept careful notes of my research, phone calls and meetings, plus copies of all correspondence. Beyond that, my educational and career paths had embedded in me a disciplined approach to learning.

I had been a college student for a long time. I spent four years getting my BS in physics at MSU. Then I took night classes my first two years in Los Alamos, getting halfway to an MS in physics. Returning to East Lansing, I invested nearly two years getting my MBA.

My job at Alexander Marketing Services also required constant learning. Unlike most ad agencies, we did not work with clients selling consumer goods, such as toothpaste, where product features and benefits were obvious.

Instead, we specialized in industrial marketing where my science background helped me understand complex products and market them to engineers, scientists, and business executives.

Although my first title at the agency was account manager, I spent much of my time writing copy for ads and brochures on products like dock levelers, ion exchange resins, and computer hardware and software.

Fortunately for me, the precise, methodical approach I used in other areas of my life served me well in the search for my personal history.

It was still January when I received another envelope from the Michigan Department of Public Health. Remembering my second request for a birth certificate using the name Richard Bojanzyk, I wondered if the ploy had worked.

Yes, it had! I now had my original birth certificate. My name on the certificate was Richard Harold Bojanzyk. Harold was my adopted father's name, but there was no way to tell who came up with "Richard."

Jackie's full name was Jacqueline Lee Hartzell. Her birthplace was Detroit and her address at the time of my birth was on Jewel Street in Lansing, my adoptive parents' apartment.

This birth certificate listed my father as Leonard Richard Bojanzyk. Leonard's presence on the document did not surprise me. Conception occurred before their divorce was final. So the law considered Jackie's former husband to be my legal father.

I was surprised to learn that Leonard's middle name was Richard. The idea of Jackie naming me after her ex-husband seemed ludicrous. I preferred to believe that my name came from Leonard's kid brother, Richard, whom she reportedly adored.

My collection of false birth certificates was growing. I had the false one that swore I was the biological offspring of my adoptive parents. And now I had one that was almost certainly half wrong, listing Leonard as my father.

I wondered if Jackie and Leonard's divorce papers might contain some worthwhile information. I called and then wrote the Wayne County Clerk's office for a copy.

Next, I received a call from Mike's aunt, Eleanor, the one who had convinced him that I was in fact his brother.

Without any prompting from me, she had appointed herself my research assistant for the Detroit area. Once again, I was amazed and pleased that people like Jeanette, Carol, and now Eleanor kept pitching in to help with my search.

Eleanor's first stop had been the funeral home in Plymouth that handled the funeral for Jackie and Joyce. She searched the home's old records without finding any paperwork on the deceased sisters.

Next, she went to Grand Lawn Cemetery. Since it was still winter, she had to wipe snow off tombstones. But she eventually found the markers for Jackie and Joyce, side by side.

The tombstones listed them as Jacqueline Hartzell and Joyce Clark. Jackie had taken back the Hartzell name after her divorce. Joyce, a year younger, was married to a Clark at the time of her death.

Records in the cemetery office showed the date of death as June 11, 1947. Jackie's age at death was twenty-one years, three months, and seventeen days.

Marion Ratkewicz had made the cemetery arrangements. The girls' mother apparently was still using her second husband's name. But Eleanor knew that Marion was living with Bill French, whom everyone called "Frenchy."

Armed with the exact date of the accident, Eleanor's final stop had been the Detroit Public Library. She checked the old newspaper records on microfilm and found articles in the *Detroit News* and the *Detroit Times*.

The accident occurred a little after midnight when the Jeep they were riding in went out of control and hit a viaduct. Joyce died instantly at the site in Oakland County. Jackie died a little later at the Northville Hospital in Wayne County.

The driver of the Jeep was Tom Martin, age twenty-nine, part owner of Cavalcade Inn. The surviving passenger was a woman named Lou Green. I assumed that was a nickname for Louise.

I had already decided that the driver of the Jeep was not a nice guy. The fact that the Martin name was not Polish gave me hope that he was not my father.

I added "Find Lou Green" to my to-do list. She might know if Jackie and Tom Martin had been romantically involved.

After thanking Eleanor for her hard work, I wrote again to the Michigan Department of Public Health. I now had enough details to request copies of Jackie's birth and death certificates.

Within a couple weeks, I had received both certificates plus the court record of her divorce from Leonard.

I learned that Jackie's father, my grandfather, was Horace Hartzell. Her mother's maiden name was Marion Garlick. Horace had worked for Michigan Bell Telephone Company.

The death certificate made me shudder a little when I read the cause of death: "Internal hemorrhage and shock following crushing injuries to chest. Auto collided with viaduct."

That description was a lot more real and personal than the simple fact that she had died.

The divorce papers provided some insights into Jackie's life. She and Leonard were married in Napoleon, Ohio on October 2, 1942, by a justice of the peace. Jackie was only sixteen, possibly too young to get married in Michigan.

I knew that Mike was not born until late October 1943. So Jackie's early marriage was not due to pregnancy.

Jackie moved out of the home she shared with Leonard in December 1944 and signed divorce papers in January 1945. Later in the divorce proceedings, she listed her employer as Wall Wire Products in Plymouth.

In April, she took Michael to his grandmother Bojanzyk's home. She testified that she had no place to keep the child with her and did not want to board him with strangers.

A Friend of the Court report revealed that Jackie had later arranged to live with her sister, Marilyn, and take Michael back. Unfortunately, Marilyn's husband was transferred to Kentucky and Jackie's plan fell through.

These details made me feel proud of Jackie. She acted in Mike's best interest and had not given up on getting him back.

The judge signed the divorce decree on December 18, 1945. He awarded Jackie custody with the understanding that Michael would remain with his grandmother until Jackie could provide a suitable home.

On the date her divorce was final, Jackie would have been four months pregnant with me. She must have known it and would soon leave the area to live with my adoptive parents in Lansing.

Shortly after receiving these documents, I had a meeting with a software client in Ann Arbor. On my way home, I decided to detour through Plymouth and Northville. I had never been to either town, but they were central to the life and death of my birth mother and possibly my birth father.

Using information from the newspaper clippings Eleanor had sent and my growing collection of legal documents, I made several stops. The first one was Plymouth High School where the Hartzell and Bojanzyk kids went to school.

I found the large boarding house where Jackie lived during her divorce proceedings and the small house on Blunk Street where she was staying when she died.

Next, I located the former site of Wall Wire Products, where Jackie worked after leaving Leonard. Then I drove by the Burroughs plant, where she was working as a shipping clerk at the time of her death.

The residential neighborhood near Plymouth Road and Stark Street, where Jackie once lived with her mother, was gone. Various commercial businesses filled the space once occupied by small homes.

Cavalcade Inn had burned down many years earlier, but by asking around, I found the site. Although the roads had changed, I also located the approximate site of the Jeep accident that killed Jackie and Joyce.

The day was a "Sentimental Journey" in every way. Seeing these places made Jackie's life far more real to me.

Before leaving the area, I stopped at the local newspapers to search for additional clippings about the accident. Amazingly, the *Northville Record* still had the actual newspapers from 1947. No microfilm.

The accident that killed Jackie and Joyce was front-page news in this small-town paper. But the article did not include any photos.

The newspaper's editor was in the office at the time. As she photocopied the article for me, she asked about my interest in that news item.

Without mentioning adoption, I told her that one of the women killed in the accident was my mother, adding that I had no pictures of her and was hoping there might have been one with the article.

The editor noted that many people in Northville and nearby Plymouth had lived in the area a long time. Perhaps one of their readers had a photo. She took my name and phone number and promised to mention my query in the next weekly issue, dated February 10, 1982.

On February 11, my phone rang. Once the woman caller confirmed she was speaking to me, she surprised me with these words: "This is your Aunt Marilyn."

15

LYNN

The voice on the other end of the line belonged to my biological aunt. Marilyn was the older sister of my birth mother, Jackie.

Of course, I was thrilled to receive her call. Marilyn, who I learned went by the nickname, Lynn, did not live near Northville. But an incredible series of events caused her to learn about me through a newspaper she did not read.

- A serious traffic accident had recently occurred in almost exactly the same spot as Jackie and Joyce's accident thirty-five years earlier.
- This reminded Lynn of her sisters' accident and she mentioned the coincidence to her daughter, Judi.
- Shortly after that conversation, Judi happened to speak with a friend who lived in Northville.
- For some reason, Judi shared the old story of her aunts' deaths with that friend.
- The next day the *Northville Record* came out with its brief note about the old accident and a son looking for a photo of his mother.

- Judi's friend happened to see the item and realized that the two sisters it mentioned had to be Judi's aunts.
- The friend called Judi and read her the article. Judi called the editor of the paper, who said I'd made a good impression on her.
- Judi then called her mother, Lynn, who immediately called me.

Fortunately, Lynn knew and remembered that Jackie had given up a child for adoption. So Lynn correctly surmised that I was that child. She was happy to introduce herself and fill me in on family history.

Lynn was the family's oldest child, born in 1923. Jackie and Joyce came along in 1926 and 1927.

Their parents were Horace and Marion Hartzell. Horace was a bright man with a good job at the telephone company. But he drank a lot and often squandered the family's money.

Tensions rose between the girls' parents until Horace left his wife and family in 1938. When he didn't return, Marion had to find a job.

Lynn was in high school and remained at home. But Marion had to board the two younger girls in the Edwin Denby Home run by the Salvation Army. Jackie and Joyce lived in that home from 1938 to 1941.

After Marion married her second husband, Johnny Ratkewicz, she was able to bring Jackie and Joyce home. Jackie, then fifteen, hated her stepfather. Lynn thought the home situation had been a factor in Jackie's decision to quit school early and marry Leonard at such a young age.

Lynn, who was three years older, also got married. She remembered spending a lot of time with Jackie in the summer of 1943. Both girls were pregnant for the first time and Jackie's husband, Leonard, was away in the service.

When Jackie and Leonard later split up, Lynn was preoccupied with her own family. She had two babies at home and did not want to get in the middle of a divorce case. Once Mike moved to his paternal grandmother's home, Lynn never saw him again.

"I did see Mike on a Detroit television station a few years ago," Lynn said. "He was a contestant on *Bowling for Dollars*. But I figured he would not know who I was, so I never contacted him."

Naturally, I wondered if Lynn would be able to name my biological father. But she could not answer that question for me.

When her husband's employer transferred him to Kentucky, Lynn followed him. She did not return until the fall of 1945 and was then dealing with her own marital problems. As a result, she had little contact with Jackie and did not know much about her sister's last two years.

She knew about Jackie's second pregnancy, but Jackie never shared anything with her about the father.

When I described myself as tall, Lynn wondered if my father might have been Lester Barney, a tall Plymouth man whose family owned a restaurant called Barneys. Jackie and Lester had dated at some time, but Lynn could not remember when.

A veteran, Lester had shrapnel in his head that gave him seizures. He never married and died in a motorcycle accident in the early 1950s.

Since Barney was not a Polish name, I did not think he could be the one. But taking detailed notes was my nature. So I wrote down the information.

After divorcing her first husband, Lynn remarried in 1948. Her second husband was the love of her life and they had four more children for a total of six—all girls. He had died some years before this conversation and she was now a widow.

I asked Lynn if she knew what happened to her sister Joyce's daughter. She knew the daughter's maiden name was Linda Clark. The last thing Lynn had heard was that Linda was divorced. But they had not been in touch for at least fifteen years, so Lynn did not know Linda's current name or where she lived.

As for my quest for a photo, Lynn had good news. She did have a photo of my mother. It was a formal studio portrait taken when Jackie was about fifteen years old. Lynn offered to have a copy made and send it to me. We ended the call with a promise to speak again soon.

A week later, I received a large envelope from Aunt Lynn. I tore into it like a five-year-old on Christmas morning.

In addition to the photo of Jackie, she also included two old studio portraits of Horace's mother, my great-grandmother. There was also a studio photo of Jackie and Lynn taken when Jackie was about a year old, and a snapshot of Marion, my grandmother.

To complete the package, Lynn had even tracked down a copy of the *Northville Record* article that resulted in her calling me. I was touched by her thoughtfulness.

As an adoptee who had never seen any biological ancestors, I pored over every photo and proudly showed them to my family and friends.

The picture that meant the most to me, of course, was the eight-by-ten black-and-white photo of Jackie, my birth mother. She was beautiful. And that wasn't just my biased opinion. Every person I showed the photo to had the same reaction. More than that, she looked happy. And I saw myself in her eyes.

Jackie at age 15

ekend after the photos arrived, I went on a two-night men's
St. Lazare Retreat House on Spring Lake. A silent retreat in a
al setting, it allowed many hours for personal reflection. In my
I used the time to dwell on my search in general and my birth
nother in particular.

I took along a couple books on adoption search that others had recommended.

It surprised me to learn that many adoptees felt angry with their birth mothers for rejecting them. I had never felt that and I wondered why. I decided it was because I learned about my adoption so late. By the age of eighteen, the fact that a young, unmarried girl could not raise a baby alone seemed obvious to me.

Other adoptees spoke of having fantasies about their birth mothers coming back into their lives. Once again, I missed that phase due to the lateness of my discovery. About to leave for college, I had been looking forward to a life with less parental supervision. I had no desire for a second mother in my life.

There were, of course, other comments in the books that matched my feelings exactly. For example, adoptees spoke of feeling more complete once they knew the facts about their background. My story was far from finished. Yet I could feel a growing contentment as the pieces fell into place.

I had taken Jackie's photo with me to the retreat house and I propped it up on the desk in my tiny room. Like most guys, I was always aware of my thoughts. But my feelings were difficult to find. That weekend, as I tried hard to get them to surface, I was more successful than I ever imagined.

After staring at Jackie for a long time, tears began to form in the corners of my eyes. Then I really started to cry. It took me much of the weekend to identify the feelings behind this sudden burst of emotion.

Why would I cry about a woman I could not possibly remember who had died when I was a year old?

When I started my search, I was merely curious about Jackie. She was more of a concept than a real person. But as I got to know more about her, the rough life she led and her tragic early death, I developed feelings for her. She wasn't just a name on a birth certificate anymore. She was my mother. And I knew I loved her.

Eventually, most children grieve over the death of their parents. I had already lost the man who had been Dad to me. Now I was experiencing delayed grief over my birth mother's death and our lost relationship.

Obviously, there were many things I never got to ask Jackie. But on that weekend, I discovered some things I wanted to tell her.

I wanted her to know that I understood why she couldn't keep me and I was not angry. That giving me up was the right thing to do in her situation. Finally, I wanted her to know that I had turned out OK.

As I continued to gaze at Jackie's photo, I thought of the movie *Somewhere in Time*, which had been filmed on Michigan's Mackinac Island. My wife, Pat, and I had seen it a little more than a year earlier.

In the movie, Christopher Reeve's character, a playwright in the late 1970s, becomes entranced with the photo of a lovely young girl (Jane Seymour) from 1912. He then uses self-hypnosis to travel back in time to meet her.

That was exactly what I wanted to do! Only I wanted to travel back to the 1940s to meet the beautiful young woman in this photo. I lay quietly on my bed, closed my eyes, and gave it my best shot.

It didn't work, of course. But I really wished it had.

———◆———

On the last Saturday in February 1982, Pat and I loaded up the kids for another first-time meeting with lost family in the Detroit suburbs. This time our destination was the home of Lynn's daughter, Judi.

We got to meet Aunt Lynn, Judi, three more of my biological cousins and many of their children. Like my meeting with Mike and Eleanor, it went quite well. I was beginning to see that there was a lot of curiosity about lost relatives from both sides of the adoption wall.

Judi presented me with an old greeting card for a baby's first birthday. It had been hers and she saved it all these years. The handwritten signature read "Aunt Jackie" and Judi wanted me to have this sample of my birth mother's handwriting.

I thought it was extremely nice of Judi to give it up for me.

When Judi learned that I had attended Michigan State in the late sixties, she remembered a strange conversation she had back then with our grandmother.

Judi was visiting Marion in a Lansing hospital, when the old woman kept insisting that she had a grandson at nearby MSU. She demanded to see him before she died.

Marion's abuse of alcohol had been legendary in the family. By that time, there were doubts about her mental health. So Judi just assumed her grandmother was hallucinating.

Now that she had met me, Judi realized that Marion was not at all crazy when she talked about a grandson at MSU.

I explained that Marion must have kept track of me through her husband Bill French's niece, Mickey Woods, who knew my adoptive parents.

Marion died in 1969—the year after I graduated. We never met.

16

TONY'S STORY

I told Mike about meeting Aunt Lynn and gave him her phone number. I also gave her Mike's number. Living less than thirty minutes from each other, I hoped they would meet. But neither one called the other. I soon realized it would be up to me to get us all together someday.

Life got busy again and I had to let my search slide for about six months. In August 1982, I got Mike to make his first visit to our home on the west side of the state. We had a great time and were starting to connect with each other.

I also stayed in touch with Aunt Lynn. We talked occasionally by phone and I stopped to see her whenever I had business in the Detroit area. She kept filling me in on her family, including her father, Horace Hartzell, who was Marion's first husband and my maternal grandfather.

Growing up, Horace had acquired the nickname "Tony," so everyone knew him by that name instead of Horace.

While Tony was still a baby, his mother had divorced his biological father, Oscar Friskie. She remarried James Hartzell, who had adopted Tony. The parents never told their son about the adoption or his mother's earlier marriage.

Once again, I was amazed at how secretive people used to be about subjects like divorce and adoption. People before my generation seemed to think that anything short of a perfect family with biological children was shameful. I just didn't get it.

When Lynn was a young girl, Oscar Friskie suddenly showed up at her family's doorstep. Tony was at work, so Oscar introduced himself to Marion. Unfortunately, he was only in Detroit for a short business trip and could not stay.

When Marion filled Tony in on Oscar's visit, my grandfather finally learned about his adoption and birth father. But Tony and Oscar never met. I wondered if I would ever meet or even identify my birth father.

That conversation with Aunt Lynn led me to ask about the nationalities on my birth mother's side. I learned that Marion's ancestors were English and Irish. Tony's mother was Pennsylvania Dutch. Tony's birth father, Oscar Friskie, had changed the family name from Janushefska. He was Polish.

I couldn't help but smile when I heard that. A great grandfather would account for one eighth of my ethnic background. If the non-identifying information on my birth father was correct, my Polack meter was now reading five-eighths Polish. Mom would be so proud.

One day I asked Aunt Lynn if she knew what happened to her father, Tony, after he disappeared in 1938. Long after the deaths of her sisters, Lynn learned that Tony had remarried in Oregon. He died in 1966, but his widow was still alive.

After getting the widow's name and phone number from Lynn, I called her in Oregon and introduced myself. Her name was Harriet Hartzell and she turned out to be one of the most fascinating characters

I had met yet. She was seventy-five then and she graciously filled me in on my grandfather's later life.

Tony was thirty-seven years old at the time he left Marion and his three daughters in Detroit. According to Harriet, Tony made his way to Kansas City and later to Salt Lake City by jumping on freight trains. The Depression was in full swing and he worked whatever jobs he could find.

Eventually, Tony made it to San Jose, California, where his parents were living in the Victorian home of his maternal grandmother. From there he moved to Oregon where he worked at a cousin's dairy. In 1940, he met Harriet, a widow, and they soon married.

According to Harriet, Tony wanted to send money for his kids in Detroit. But he wasn't earning much and he was also afraid Marion would make trouble for him if she knew where he was.

When Tony received a letter from someone telling him about the 1947 accident that killed two of his daughters, he was quite shaken up.

"He loved them all," Harriet said. "Yet Jackie was his favorite." Tony had known about Jackie's son, Mike, but not about me.

Tony was intelligent and eventually got his career going with a major manufacturing company in Portland, Oregon. Later in life, he even stopped drinking. Just days before his retirement, he died in a traffic accident.

Harriet described Tony as a good-looking man with lots of personality and a wonderful sense of humor. He attracted a lot of attention from the ladies, and Harriet had to fight off more than one woman to keep her man.

Wistfully, Harriet quoted me a line from the old song, "Thanks for the Memory." She insisted it was a perfect description of life with Tony.

"You might have been a headache but you never were a bore."

Harriet sent me two eight-by-ten photos of Tony. In one he was a young man, possibly still in his twenties, and in the other he was in his sixties. This was the first time I had ever seen pictures of a male ancestor. Everyone I showed them to thought we had features in common.

I continued to correspond with Harriet at least once a year. She wrote long, elegant letters about anything and everything. She was bright, charming, and more than a little eccentric.

Much like Mike's Aunt Eleanor, she was not a relative of mine. Yet she was still excited that I had contacted her and was eager to share whatever she could to help me.

My next clue did not come from Harriet, however. It was a small, black-and-white photograph that got me excited.

17

RAY

In late summer 1982, I passed through Lansing on a business trip and stopped to see Carol Woods. That wasn't her married name, of course, but she would always be Carol Woods to me.

Members of her mother's family had given me the information on my birth mother. I wanted to fill Carol in on my progress and it was a timely stop, as she was anxious to show me something.

Since those family members had refused to identify a relative rumored to be my father, Carol decided to hunt up some old family photos and make her own guess.

She showed me a small snapshot of a man leaning against a car. He was tall and slender with nearly black hair. Although the photo was too small to see the details of his face, there was something about him that reminded me of myself.

His name was Ray Bonie. He was the brother of Bill French's first wife, Marie, whom Bill left to be with my grandmother, Marion. Carol described him as a handsome playboy known to date a lot of girls.

I told Carol that my non-identifying information claimed my biological father was Polish. The Bonie family, originally spelled Boni, was Italian.

Yet how could I know for sure that the name and nationality in my file were correct? The court staff would have recorded whatever Jackie told them. I was sure nobody checked this stuff. What if Jackie also had been protecting the same man?

I thought Mr. Bonie was worth a look.

Fortunately, Jeanette also lived in Lansing. So I dropped off Ray's photo to her. About a week later, she called to report that she had tracked down Ray and had spoken with him by phone.

She told me Ray remembered Jackie's mother, Marion, right away because he once found her with Bill French at a bar on the corner of Plymouth and Stark. As Jeanette told me this, I thought that intersection sounded familiar. Then I remembered it was near Marion's home.

Since Bill was married to his sister, Marie, Ray was not happy finding him with Marion. He pummeled Bill, ran Marion out of the bar, and told his sister what happened.

As his conversation with Jeanette continued, Ray admitted knowing Jackie. But he did not remember ever going out with her. Nor had he heard any rumor placing someone in his family with her.

Ray was quite clear about one thing, however. If he thought for a minute that he had a son somewhere, he would be right there.

After years of adoption search work, Jeanette could usually tell when people were lying to her. She was convinced that Ray was telling the truth. He was not my father and this was another dead end.

Late in 1982, I was able to check off another item on my to-do list. I took what Aunt Lynn could tell me about her sister Joyce's in-laws and tracked down my biological cousin, Linda. Speaking to her by phone, I learned she was divorced with three children and lived in a Detroit suburb.

Linda's father had never said much about the accident that killed her mother, Joyce, and my mother, Jackie. He was away in the Navy when it happened.

In February 1983, I arranged a Hartzell reunion of sorts. Linda hosted the event at her home. Pat and I brought our kids and picked up Aunt Lynn. Mike brought his girlfriend. The day went well, but no one seemed as excited about it as I was.

That same winter Eleanor obtained a current phone number for her brother, Leonard, in California. I wanted to confirm that he was not my father, so I asked Jeanette to call him for me.

Leonard was hostile when he answered, wondering how she got his number. Anticipating a reaction like this, Jeanette gave him a line about Jackie's second son needing medical information about his father.

Leonard said Jackie dated a lot of guys and he had no idea who the father was. He had stayed on his side of town. His account matched what everyone else had said. So it seemed certain that Mike's father was not also my father.

When Eleanor heard about the call, she joked that it was a good thing Jeanette caught Leonard off guard. If he had time to think about it, her brother might have claimed to be my father just to hit me up for money. Remembering Mike's comments about his father, I had to agree.

Following a suggestion from Jeanette, I wrote a letter to the probate court in late 1983. I explained that I now knew the name of my birth mother and enclosed my original birth certificate as proof.

I also informed them that Jackie was no longer living and included a copy of her death certificate. My letter mentioned the name of my brother, Mike, and noted that I had met him.

My point was this: since my birth mother's privacy was no longer an issue, they could reveal more about what was in my file.

Eight weeks went by without a response. Then in late January 1984, I received a detailed letter from the probate court judge. He shared everything they had on Jackie's life. It matched and confirmed what I had already learned from others. But he did provide some new information about the man Jackie named as my birth father.

According to my file, he was a coworker at her place of employment. They dated for six months, she became pregnant, and, shortly after that, they split up. Jackie said he was not ready to marry after serving in the armed forces so long.

The coworker reference was a big clue. I already knew some places in Plymouth where Jackie had worked: Wall Wire Products and Cavalcade Inn. At the time of her death, she worked at Burroughs. But I was pretty sure she only got that job after I was born.

Now I could narrow my search to men with whom she worked. It was time for another trip to Plymouth.

18

PLYMOUTH

On a Saturday in February 1984, I got an early start and made my second trip to Plymouth, the small town where my birth mother had lived. My first stop was the Plymouth Historical Library, where I browsed through city directories from the 1940s.

I scanned each directory for men with Polish names who worked at Wall Wire. There were a lot of them. Most were plant or office workers. But I also found a vice president named Max Wachowiak.

Wall Wire was gone by 1957. According to the librarian, the company had relocated to Tennessee. So that particular search came to an abrupt end.

As expected, I confirmed that Tom Martin, the driver of the Jeep when Jackie was killed, was associated with Cavalcade Inn. But I didn't find any obviously Polish names who worked there.

The librarian was sure that a former Cavalcade Inn manager had a Polish name, but she couldn't remember it. She said he later became manager of a restaurant called Nicki's.

While at the historical library, I got the idea of looking up classmates of Jackie's in the 1944 Plymouth High School yearbook. That would have been her class, had she stayed in school. I compared names with the current local telephone directory to see who might still be in the area.

I called a few of them. Some remembered Jackie, but no one knew anything about her after she left high school. That seemed reasonable. Jackie had jumped into adulthood quickly, getting married at sixteen and having Mike at seventeen. I doubt that she had time to stay in touch with friends who were still in high school.

My next stop was Plymouth Township Hall. I wanted to know if there were any old records that would list owners of Cavalcade Inn. There were not. But someone suggested I talk to Ralph Lorenz, owner of the Mayflower Hotel. A longtime Plymouth resident, Mr. Lorenz had been active in the local business community for decades.

I had noticed that big old hotel as I drove through downtown. Since it wasn't far away, I decided to pay Mr. Lorenz a visit. Fortunately, he was in and someone directed me to his office. A large man in his seventies, he invited me to sit down.

Mr. Lorenz told me that brothers Walt and Earl Smith once owned Cavalcade Inn. Walt had died. But Earl was alive and now a wealthy man who owned bars, theaters, and a bowling alley. He would probably know the history of prior owners. He gave me Earl's phone number.

As for Wall Wire, Mr. Lorenz had known some of the company's executives. Most were deceased now. But Max Wachowiak was still alive and had retired to Sun City, Arizona.

As I drove home, I wondered again if the description of the short, blond Polish man in my file might refer to my legal father, Leonard Bojanzyk, instead of my birth father. Since the judge had responded so freely to my last inquiry, I decided to write him a follow-up letter.

In March 1984, the judge wrote back with the following, definitive answer:

"The records are absolutely clear that this is the description of your biological father. If that were also the description of Leonard Bojanzyk, it is a remarkable coincidence and one which I cannot explain."

I was glad to clear that up. Maybe the coincidence was not so surprising after all. Men and women are often drawn to new partners who have the same physical traits that attracted them before. And there was certainly no shortage of Polish men in the suburbs of Detroit.

On a Monday night in April, I decided to call Earl Smith, whom Ralph Lorenz had said was a former owner of Cavalcade Inn.

By then, I had developed a simplified introduction for interviewing people outside the family. I avoided the entire adoption story and just said I was researching my family history. My mother had died when I was a baby and I grew up outside the area. So I was now contacting people who might have known her.

After listening to their memories of Jackie, I would casually mention that my father's identity was unknown and I was hoping to meet him or at least learn something about him. That comment opened the door to discuss the men in her life.

Earl told me he had worked at Lingeman Products, a small manufacturing company next door to Cavalcade Inn. He remembered that Jackie's sister, Joyce, also had worked there for awhile.

He spent a lot of time at Cavalcade Inn and remembered Jackie working as a waitress. He also remembered the accident that killed her and Joyce.

Tom Martin, the driver of the Jeep, was then the owner of Cavalcade Inn. After the 1947 accident, he sold the bar to a couple named Robinson who, in 1952, sold it to Earl and his brother, Walt. Tom Martin eventually moved to California, where he did extremely well in the furniture business.

I asked Earl if he remembered Lou (possibly Louise) Green, the fourth passenger in the Jeep. He did. She was part of a clique of girls— including Jackie and Joyce—that ran around together. She married a local guy and moved to California.

Then I asked Earl if he knew the name of a Polish guy from Cavalcade Inn who later managed Nicki's. He knew that, too. The man's name was Art Kopersky.

Earl suggested I call Ronnie Phillips, who used to work for Tom Martin and was still in the area.

That was my next call and I caught Ronnie at home. He remembered Cavalcade Inn well. It was the place to go in the forties and a regular crowd was there two or three nights a week.

He said Jackie only worked at the bar part time. That made sense to me, since I knew she also worked at Wall Wire.

Ronnie said Jackie and Joyce were constant companions and both were especially attractive. Unfortunately for me, he could not remember Jackie dating anyone who worked at the bar.

Ronnie remembered Lou Green, too. She married a man named Norm Niles. Ronnie thought they'd lived in California once, but he was sure they had returned to the Northville area.

This got me excited. Lou Green was a friend of Jackie's and a survivor of the Jeep crash that took her life. I called information and got a phone number for Norm Niles in Northville.

Lou answered the phone. Yes, she remembered Jackie. How could she forget, having been a passenger in the crash that took her life?

She, Jackie, and Joyce had been together that day. They ran into Tom Martin at the Northville Hotel bar. He invited them to ride with him to Walled Lake, which had a big bar and was about ten miles north of Northville. That was how they happened to be together in the Jeep that day. Lou was pretty sure that Jackie and Tom were not a couple.

Lou described Jackie as a wonderful, beautiful girl with blue eyes and hair that was almost black. Both Jackie and Joyce were exceptionally nice people.

She had not known Jackie long, but knew she was divorced. Lou added that Jackie never mentioned anything about having kids.

Lou also confirmed Aunt Lynn's recollection that Jackie had dated Lester Barney, the man who, Aunt Lynn had told me, died in a motorcycle accident. She remembered Jackie seeing a couple other guys who rode motorcycles: Mark Russick, who also died riding, and Jerry Jarskey, who was later electrocuted in his basement during a thunderstorm.

Lou could not remember when she first met Jackie. But the overall impression I got was that Lou only knew Jackie after I was born and Jackie had returned to Plymouth. The men she associated with Jackie had dated my mother too late to be my father and were too dead to be interviewed.

After all this research, I still could not determine who Jackie was seeing in August 1945 when she got pregnant with me.

I asked about Art Kopersky, the Polish man from Cavalcade Inn. Lou remembered him from Nicki's. He now had a nice place in Northern Michigan. Although Art was a short Polish man, he was pudgy and not at all handsome. Lou could not imagine Jackie with him.

Lou suggested that her husband, Norm, might know more. So she put him on the phone and I brought him up to date on the reason for my call.

Norm said Jackie was the most beautiful girl around. But he knew nothing about her social life.

However, he knew a great deal about the bar business. Art Kopersky was a shrewd businessman. He acquired the liquor license from Cavalcade Inn and, with partners from Northville Downs racetrack, built a place called Thunderbird. Norm had heard that Art then moved north where he got involved in a "really nice" restaurant.

I mentioned to Norm that Earl Smith thought that he and Lou were in California. Norm and Lou had indeed lived there for awhile, but they liked it better back here. Then Norm surprised me with this question.

"Did you know Earl Smith murdered his wife in the Cavalcade Inn?"

I had just talked to the man earlier that evening. Not surprisingly, he had not mentioned that incident.

From what Norm then told me, Earl's wife was running around with another man. Earl, learning they were together at the bar that evening, walked in with a shotgun and shot her dead in front of witnesses. Earl had a good lawyer, however, and managed to avoid jail. Today he is a multimillionaire. Go figure.

"Well," I said. "He seemed like a nice guy on the phone." As far as I knew, Earl Smith was the first murderer I'd spoken with.

I then asked Norm about Wall Wire Products. Norm recommended that I call Bill Fann. Bill had been a foreman and union leader at the plant. He followed the company when it moved to Tennessee. He gave me Bill's home number and told me to tell him that Norm and Lou suggested I call.

I had been on the phone all evening. So I waited until the following Sunday, April 15, 1984, and made the call. I reached Bill Fann's wife. She had grown up with Norm and Lou. She told me Bill was in

Michigan visiting a sister who was ill. I left my number and asked that Bill call me collect after he returned to Tennessee.

Bill never called me back and I soon forgot about my attempt to reach him.

Numerous other things pushed their way to the top of my personal to-do list. Before I realized it, five and a half years slipped by. It would take another surprise phone call to light my fire again.

19

FAMILY BONDS

In spite of my success in reuniting with and learning about my birth mother's family, I still didn't know the identity of my birth father. Yet from 1984 to 1989, the activities of the present once again consumed my life.

My career was going well. I had become a vice president at my ad agency and had earned Certified Business Communicator status through the Business Marketing Association.

Our family was growing up and staying busy. In 1989, Jenny turned sixteen and the twins were eleven.

Whenever possible, I was molding my work schedule to fit around our kids' activities. Whether it was sports, concerts, Scouting events, or parent-teacher conferences, I was in attendance 90 percent of the time. If I was not out of town, I was there.

My perseverance probably sprang from the lack of such fatherly involvement when I was a child. Dad's afternoon shift in Lansing prevented him from attending any of my weekday activities in Ionia. Plus, there were a lot of years when the auto industry was booming and he worked overtime on Saturdays, as well.

Mom did her best to make up for Dad's absence. A full-time home-maker until I was in high school, she never missed anything I was involved in. And Mom didn't just show up to watch. She pitched in to help.

She was a room mother in elementary school and a den mother for my Cub Scout troop. During my four years of high school band, she found time to manage the care and storage of 140 band uniforms.

My wife, Pat, was also a full-time homemaker in an era when that was far less common. So between us, we spent a lot time at the kids' schools and athletic fields.

Besides keeping up with our children, I wanted to build a relation-ship with my new brother, Mike. Yet his schedule was just as packed as mine was. Besides teaching elementary school physical education, he ran his school's latchkey program, keeping dozens of kids busy in the gym before and after school.

At certain times of the year, he also taught driver's training on eve-nings and weekends. Beyond that, Mike's bachelor life was full of ongo-ing commitments to golf and softball leagues in the warmer months and bowling leagues and ski club trips in the winter.

In addition to our enormous scheduling conflicts, it was a two-and-a-half-hour drive—each way—between our homes in the suburbs of Detroit and Grand Rapids. So visits to each other's homes continued to be rare.

To ensure at least a minimum relationship, Pat and I started meeting Mike and his girlfriend for dinner once or twice a year at some midpoint, often in Lansing.

I still didn't feel like I really knew my brother. So I found a way to build the relationship I wanted. I took up golf again.

Golf had never been my thing. After learning the sport in college, I had played about a dozen times in my life. I had given it up completely many years before I met Mike.

Knowing Mike loved the game, I decided that I would learn to love it, too. I made a couple trips to a driving range and called Mike to tell him I was ready to play. Mike then planned a three-day golf trip for the two of us in northern Michigan.

Mike reserved a motel room in the golfing mecca of Gaylord and scheduled our tee times at three different courses. This was the first time we ever spent that much time together, so it was definitely a bonding experience. Plus, the following incident provided Mike with something to tease me about for the rest of my life.

My prior golf experience had been on relatively easy, wide open golf courses. Plus, my memories of golf were somewhat hazy by then. So it seemed reasonable to me that buying a sleeve of three golf balls was adequate preparation for the long weekend.

The golf courses Mike picked in northern Michigan turned out to be a lot more difficult than those I remembered. The fairways were narrow ribbons of grass surrounded on three sides by dense woods. The view from tee to green was often like staring into a tunnel.

Somewhere on the second hole, I ran out of balls.

When Mike learned that I had only brought three balls for fifty-four holes of golf, he thought his new brother was the craziest optimist he had ever known.

In the following years, golf provided Mike and me with some much-needed common ground. At least once a year, we would meet somewhere to play golf.

Since I usually required a couple extra strokes per hole, Mike was extraordinarily patient with me. He offered tips when he thought it would help. But he knew I would never play more than a few times a year. He accepted me as I was.

On the other hand, there would be one or two holes per game on which he struggled and the ball bounced well for me. When I happened to tie him or even win a hole, he was always good natured about it.

As my son, Mark, grew older, Mike and I began to include him. Mark has a natural athleticism that I lack and it wasn't long before he was playing closer to his Uncle Mike's level than to mine.

As an adoptee, I think a lot about the questions of nature versus nurture. Do our genes predetermine certain traits? Or is our childhood environment a bigger factor?

Even though we had the same mother, Mike was a more natural athlete than I was, even choosing physical education as a career. His father,

Leonard, had been a star athlete in high school. If Mike inherited his athletic abilities from his father, did that mean my biological father was the captain of the chess club?

On the other hand, Mike and I also had vastly different childhood environments. Raised mostly by his grandparents, Mike grew up in the same household with a young uncle, Richard, who was more like a big brother.

I didn't see my Dad much, because of his work schedule. And none of my uncles or cousins lived in Ionia. Besides, Dad was fifty years old by the time I was ten. He taught me things that were popular with men his age—to bowl, fish, and shoot a gun—but not to pitch a baseball or throw a football.

I wondered the same thing about my own children. All three were good at sports. Had they inherited some kind of athlete's gene from Pat's family? Or was their athletic success merely the result of our taking the time to involve them in so many sports at an early age?

While thoughts like this fluttered into my head from time to time, the actual search for my birth father simmered on life's back burner. Then, a few days after Thanksgiving in November 1989, I received an unexpected phone call from Jeanette.

The founder of Adoptees Search for Knowledge, Jeanette had been my primary search adviser and was the one who found Mike through his Uncle Richard and then his Aunt Eleanor. Jeanette and I had not talked in years, but I recognized her voice immediately.

"Are you still interested in finding your birth father?" she asked.

"Of course," I replied. Her next sentence got my attention. "Then I have good news for you," she said.

20

BACK IN GEAR

Although the engine of desire was still there, my search had been idling in neutral for more than five years. Jeanette's call kicked things back into gear.

Since we last talked, Jeanette had completed her own search and found her son. But she never stopped helping adoptees and other birth parents. And many of them, like me, had sealed adoption files in Lansing's Ingham County Probate Court.

Jeanette had convinced the judge to test a confidential intermediary program. It was the first such program in the state of Michigan.

If an adult adoptee petitioned the court to participate in this program, the judge would let Jeanette read the adoption file to learn the identities of that person's birth parents.

Acting as an agent of the court, Jeanette could not divulge this information to the adoptee. But she could use it to track down a birth parent. If she was successful—and the birth parent agreed—Jeanette could then put the birth parent and adoptee in touch with each other.

Jeanette had already done this twenty-seven times for adoptees currently in search. Now she was going back through her cold files and decided to call me. She charged one hundred and fifty dollars for her time plus expenses. She wanted to know if I was interested.

I probably thought a whole microsecond about that before I heartily agreed. Jeanette told me how to phrase my request and I wrote my next letter to the probate court judge.

This process would not guarantee success, of course. Once Jeanette learned my birth father's name, she still had to find him. She had a lot of experience tracking people down. But could she locate this man forty-three years after my birth? Would he still be alive? And would he agree to speak with me?

Anxious to do more than just wait, I dug out my old search notes to see where I left off. I made a list of people to contact and questions to ask.

When my search stalled out in 1984, I had been trying to reach Bill Fann. He had been a union leader at Wall Wire Products and I had hoped he might remember Jackie and any co-workers she dated. Now it was December 1989 and no one answered his Tennessee number.

I had gotten Bill's name and number from Norm Niles, the husband of Lou Green. I tried to call Norm and Lou, but someone else now had that phone number.

I asked Jeanette for help and she soon confirmed that both Bill Fann and Norm Niles had died. She could not find Lou Green.

Another person on my list was Jackie's landlord, the man who owned the rooming house where she lived in 1945. I had discovered his name through the city directories, but had never gotten around to calling him. Now I reached his home and learned that he, too, had died a few months earlier. The widow had not been around Plymouth when Jackie was alive.

I began to berate myself for letting my search slide for five years. Many of Jackie's contemporaries were now deceased. And those who survived to retirement may have moved to warmer climates.

That thought reminded me of Max Wachowiak, the vice president at Wall Wire Products. He had retired to Sun City, Arizona. His Polish name had caught my eye, since my non-identifying information had my birth father as Polish. Plus, the judge had written that my father worked with Jackie.

I checked long-distance information and found that name in Sun City. I called and spoke to the man who answered.

I had found the right guy. Max had joined Wall Wire in 1947. So he'd started too late to overlap with Jackie's 1945 employment. He did not remember hearing her name. He did tell me that the company employed about two hundred people back then.

Most of the hourly people belonged to the International Association of Machinists union. He suggested I contact the union headquarters in Wisconsin to see if they had any employee records. I added that to my to-do list.

In addition to her full-time job at Wall Wire, Jackie had worked part time as a waitress at Cavalcade Inn. The only Polish coworker I had uncovered there was a manager named Art Kopersky.

Five years ago, Norm Niles had told me that Art was involved in a nice restaurant up north. But he didn't know the name of it.

The previous summer, Pat and I had dined up north at the Brookside Inn in Beulah, Michigan. We noticed a posted article that said the owner was Kirk Lorenz. The name caught my eye, because I had interviewed Ralph Lorenz, who owned the Mayflower Hotel in Plymouth.

If Kirk were also from Plymouth, he might know which northern Michigan restaurant Art Kopersky was involved in. I called the Brookside Inn and asked to speak with Kirk.

Sure enough, Kirk was Ralph's son. The Lorenz name was Austrian. He had heard of Art Kopersky. Art's northern Michigan place had been the Sandtrap Restaurant at the Grand Traverse Resort.

I knew that name. The Grand Traverse Resort was famous for "The Bear," a well-known golf course designed by Jack Nicklaus. Neither Mike nor I had ever played there. It was much too difficult for me and too expensive for both of us.

Kirk went on to tell me that Art had returned to the Detroit area. He did not know him well enough to have the phone number.

Checking information for the Detroit area, I confirmed that Art had a phone, but it was an unlisted number. I then called the Sandtrap Restaurant. But it was located at the golf course and closed for the winter.

I passed all this information to Jeanette. If the Polish name in my file turned out to be Kopersky, she would know to look in the Detroit area.

I remembered Mike's Aunt Eleanor telling me that Jackie was seeing the owner of the bar where she worked. Tom Martin, the man responsible for my mother's death, had owned Cavalcade Inn when Jackie was alive. Yet no one else I had talked to ever saw the two of them as a couple. And he wasn't Polish.

Still, I decided it was time to interview Tom Martin before he, too, was dead. If Jackie had been involved with someone who worked at Cavalcade, Tom would have known about it.

Earl Smith had told me that Tom had moved to California and had done well in the furniture business. I searched some business directories in my company's library and eventually found his home phone number.

In hindsight, I should have let Jeanette make the call. But I had become so comfortable and successful at interviewing people that I felt confident enough to make the call myself.

A woman answered, presumably his wife. She sounded pleasant enough. But when I asked for Tom, she asked who was calling. I gave her my name. I could hear them talking in the background. Tom did not recognize my name, of course, and sounded annoyed by the interruption.

When Tom got on the phone, I confirmed that he was the Tom Martin who had owned Cavalcade Inn in Michigan back in the 1940s. I then gave him my usual spiel about trying to contact people who knew my mother. But when I told him Jackie's name, he claimed he did not remember her.

I reminded him of the Jeep accident involving Jackie and her sister, Joyce. He said he did not know what I was talking about and he could not help me.

Jeanette would have known what to say next. But I didn't have a clue, so the conversation ended. I had blown my chance to learn something useful from him.

I reported my failure to Jeanette. If we still needed information, Jeanette would call back later and try to catch his wife alone. Women are often more sympathetic than men, she said.

Jeanette had not yet heard from the court regarding my request for her confidential intermediary service. But she promised to let me know when the process got started.

With Christmas approaching, I decided to be patient and wait. On December 22, 1989, I received a letter from the judge. He had approved my request and authorized Jeanette to access my adoption file.

That same evening Jeanette called me with some of the most heart-thumping news I'd received in many years. She had read my file and knew the name of the man Jackie had listed as my birth father

21

CONRAD

Due to her position as an agent of the court, Jeanette could not yet tell me the man's name. It was indeed Polish but different from all the names we had found. Jackie had described him as a coworker at Wall Wire. Based on information in the file, he would now be about seventy years old. Jeanette would start looking for him the next day.

Observing a family custom, Pat and I spent New Year's Eve at home playing cards and board games with the kids. The eighties were almost over. At midnight it would be 1990.

Early in the evening, the phone rang unexpectedly. It was Jeanette. She had tracked down and contacted my birth father. Best of all, he had agreed to speak with me and now she could tell me his name. It was Conrad Perzyk.

In terms of raw excitement, this call ranked right up there with her call eight years earlier when she told me she had reached my brother's aunt, who remembered me.

Jeanette certainly had my attention and I urged her to fill me in on the details.

Conrad lived in Adrian, Michigan, about seventy miles southwest of Detroit. He was, indeed, just five foot eight inches tall, as described in my file. He had brown eyes and his hair had darkened over the years to dark brown. Born in 1919, he had been seven years older than Jackie.

Conrad had indeed dated Jackie in 1945. But he never worked at Wall Wire. They worked together at a bar where he was a bartender and Jackie was a waitress.

"But Jackie told the court they worked together at Wall Wire," I protested. Jeanette's reply was direct.

"She lied."

"Your file also says that Jackie was concerned about losing custody of Mike due to this out-of-wedlock pregnancy. I suspect she lied to avoid further damage to her reputation. Waitressing in a bar was not considered respectable employment for women back then."

"So they both worked at Cavalcade Inn," I suggested.

"No," replied Jeanette. "Conrad remembers Cavalcade Inn and even hung out there some, because they had a band and dancing. But he never worked there. And he did not meet Jackie there."

Jeanette continued. "The bar where he and Jackie worked together was on the southwest corner of Plymouth and Stark, just outside of Plymouth in Livonia Township. He can't remember the name."

Something sounded familiar about that intersection. Later, when I checked my notes, I found an earlier reference to the same bar. Ray Bonie had caught his sister's husband, Bill French, there with Jackie's mother, Marion. Ray had not remembered the name of the bar either.

My notes also reminded me that Jackie's mother had lived a few blocks northeast of that same intersection. After her breakup with Leonard, Jackie moved back in with Marion for awhile. So the bar would have been an easy walk from their home and a convenient place for Jackie to get her first job.

"Good grief," I said to Jeanette. "When I learned that Jackie had worked at Cavalcade Inn at the time of her death, I just assumed she also worked there before my birth."

"Never assume," replied Jeanette.

She and I discussed the facts some more and were able to construct a scenario that made sense.

After leaving Leonard in December 1944, Jackie worked two jobs: full-time at Wall Wire and weekends at this bar at Plymouth and Stark. After discovering she was pregnant in late 1945, she quit both jobs and moved to Lansing before her pregnancy showed.

Not wanting to field questions about where she had been for so long, Jackie would have made a fresh start when she returned to Plymouth after my birth in May 1946. She got a full-time job at Burroughs and began waitressing part time at Cavalcade Inn. We already knew those were the places she was working at the time of the accident.

I then asked Jeanette when I could speak with Conrad. She told me he had suggested that I call tomorrow after the Rose Bowl game was over.

Michigan is playing USC, I thought. I hope this doesn't mean he's another Michigan fan.

The next day I also watched the Rose Bowl. I always root for Big Ten teams—even Michigan—in bowl games. But my heart wasn't in it. The game didn't involve my Spartans, who had beaten USC in that bowl game two years earlier. Plus, I had an important call to make and the game seemed to crawl.

The game ended with Michigan on the losing end of the score. Not knowing if Conrad was watching the game at home or not, I waited another thirty minutes and then called the number Jeanette had given me.

A woman answered, presumably his wife. She said Conrad was out and her voice sounded cool. I gave her my name and said I would try again later.

On my second try, Conrad answered the phone. It was January 1, 1990, and I was finally speaking with the man my mother had named as my birth father.

Conrad was friendly and approachable. Jeanette had already told him that Jackie named him as my father in the adoption records. So I filled him in on how I happened to search for my roots.

In my logical mind, the next thing to establish was that our alleged father-son relationship could be true. But asking a complete stranger if he had been sexually intimate with your mother seemed awfully direct.

I worded my question more delicately, asking him if it were physically possible that he could be my father. He said it was and went on to tell me his story.

Conrad had quit school after the tenth grade and joined the National Guard. After the Japanese attacked Pearl Harbor, his unit was called to active duty. He spent most of World War II at a radar installation in the Aleutian Islands of Alaska. He was a sergeant.

Since those islands were considered a combat zone in the Army's points system, he qualified for a discharge before the war ended. In August 1945, he got his first post-war job as a bartender at the tavern on the corner of Plymouth and Stark. He had never mixed a drink in his life, but he started working on a Saturday night and learned on the job.

That's where he met Jackie. She was one of five waitresses who worked on weekends. After a couple weekends of working together, Conrad asked Jackie out. They dated for a few months. He was crazy about her and even took her to meet his parents. At one point, he asked her to marry him.

She turned him down. The painful breakup from her husband was still fresh and she was not ready to take another chance on marriage.

Besides, she was enjoying life as an attractive, single woman. Although she liked Conrad, she refused to date him exclusively and continued to go out with other men. Wanting a more lasting relationship than she did, Conrad broke up with her.

"When did she tell you she was pregnant?" I asked.

"Never," he replied. "She just stopped working at the bar and I never saw her or heard from her again."

Conrad only learned of the pregnancy when one of Jackie's girlfriends stopped by to tell him. His response was direct.

"If she thinks it's mine, she knows where to find me."

He never heard from Jackie. But he did hear about her death in the Jeep accident.

Conrad's story made it clear that Jackie had not been completely truthful with the court. Besides her obvious lie about Conrad being a coworker at Wall Wire, she had stretched the relationship to six months and claimed Conrad was the one who wasn't ready to marry.

Jackie's modifications to the story all made her look better. The fear of losing custody of Mike apparently weighed heavily on her testimony.

Conrad and I continued to talk for awhile, filling each other in on our lives and families. Since he never had any children, he said he would be thrilled to have a son.

That meant a lot to me. I knew that some birth parents did not appreciate being found by the children they had conceived. I had been praying for a positive reception—and it looked like my search would turn out to be a good thing for everyone involved.

I learned that Conrad had worked most of his career as an industrial engineer. He had even worked at the General Tire plastics plant in Ionia from 1978 to 1980.

That surprised me. But Conrad never lived in my hometown. When he was working in Ionia, he lived in Lowell, another small town about fifteen miles to the west.

Conrad's lifelong hobby had been ballroom dancing. He had spent much of his free time in ballrooms until his wife had to quit for health reasons three years earlier. He also played the organ.

Once again, I thought about nature versus nurture. I could dance and had played saxophone in high school. But I was barely average at both pursuits. If my birth father had a gene for dancing or music, I never got it.

Conrad was still active in retirement. He bowled twice a week in the winter and played golf in the summer. I envisioned a great foursome: my father, my brother, my son, and myself.

We agreed to meet the following Sunday, January 7, 1990, at a restaurant called Bummies in Adrian. Excitedly, I marked it on my calendar and counted down the days.

22

DOUBTS

When I returned to work the next business day, I called City Hall in Livonia. I figured someone there could find out the name of the bar that had occupied the corner of Plymouth and Stark in the 1940s. The person I spoke with promised to look into it.

Coming out of a meeting that afternoon, I found a pink phone-message slip on my desk with the following message from Livonia City Hall: "The name of the bar at that corner was Dann's Tavern."

I smiled, wondering what our receptionist must have thought when she took that call.

Sunday came and Pat and I decided to leave the kids at home for our trip to Adrian. This was more of a fact-finding mission than a social event. We could end up sitting in the restaurant all afternoon. If Conrad were indeed my father, there would be other opportunities for them to meet him.

We arrived at Bummies a little early, choosing a booth where we could watch the door and wait for Conrad to arrive.

I was anxious. Even though he was much shorter, I hoped to see something of myself in his face. I wanted an instant jolt of recognition where I could say without a doubt that this man was my father.

It didn't happen.

At the scheduled time, a short man of average build walked in and scanned the room with his eyes. His behavior told me it had to be him. But his looks said nothing.

I walked toward him and he smiled. I confirmed it was Conrad and we shook hands. He joined us in the booth where Pat and I sat on one side and he sat across from us.

The lack of physical resemblance was not a problem, I told myself. Lots of men don't look much like their fathers. We are, after all, a blend of both parents.

After the waitress took our lunch orders, Conrad apologized for meeting at the restaurant instead of his home. His wife was fearful that I was out to rob her of Conrad's estate. He felt she would accept me eventually, but she had high blood pressure and was in poor health. He did not want to upset her by bringing me to the house.

I assured him that I had no such intentions and suggested there might be some kind of legal document I could sign to eliminate her fears. Conrad said that would not be necessary.

The first thing we did was share pictures. I had brought Jackie's photo, so Conrad could confirm that she was the one he had dated. I also gave him some photos of myself as a child and as a younger man. Conrad gave me two photos of himself, one of them from roughly the time of my birth.

Since there was no overall similarity in our appearance, we focused on the minutia of hair, eyes, noses, chins, and ears. We found some common features, but I feared that might have been as much from wishful thinking as any real resemblance.

I was disappointed that we did not look more alike, but I kept my feelings to myself.

Conrad retold the story of meeting Jackie at the bar when he took the bartending job. She only worked on Saturday nights.

I asked if the name of the bar was Dann's Tavern. He had not heard that name since he'd left the job more than forty years ago, but after hearing "Dann's," he confirmed that was it.

Conrad told us again how he loved Jackie, but she had continued to go out with other guys and would not marry him.

They did not have any common friends that he could remember. Conrad noted that he and Jackie were both heavy drinkers. I mentioned that Jackie's mother and father both had their problems with alcohol. So that didn't surprise me about her.

Then Conrad revealed that he was an alcoholic. He had been clean, however, since 1963.

I had heard that alcoholism was partly genetic. With all the alcoholics in my family tree, I wondered how I had dodged that bullet. A light drinker, I had never been drunk in my life.

Conrad then told us about his family. He had a sister three years older and a brother ten years younger. At five foot eight, Conrad was the tallest one in his family. His father had been five foot six.

My mind struggled with that fact. For decades, the birth father of my fantasies had been a tall man.

One of my goals had been to get some medical history. So Conrad filled me in on his health issues and those of his parents and siblings.

I noticed some small coincidences in Conrad's personal history. Like my adoptive father, Conrad had been a member of the Elks Club. And like my adoptive mother and my wife, Conrad's mother and sister had been beauticians.

After nearly two hours together, Conrad told me he would be proud to have me as a son. I said the same about him as a father. It looked like my search was going to have a perfect ending.

But then Conrad voiced his doubts.

"I have to tell you," he said, "I don't know if it's possible for me to be your father."

"Why is that?" I asked.

"Because," he noted glumly, "I believe I've been sterile since World War II."

Conrad went on to explain that he had been married a total of four times. Even through his last three wives all had children in prior marriages, he could never father a child.

He had long ago concluded that his lengthy exposure to radar emissions was the cause. If that were true, he was already sterile by the time he met Jackie.

Before I could absorb this depressing news, Conrad had a suggestion. "I think we should do the test that Coleman Young did."

Coleman Young was the first African-American mayor of Detroit. A former girlfriend had sued him for child support for her six-year-old son, and a DNA test recently had confirmed that Coleman was the father.

Thanks to extensive news coverage, just about everyone in Michigan had heard about DNA testing.

I had to agree that Conrad was right. He had a good reason to be skeptical. And I wanted to be absolutely certain I had found my birth father. Jackie had lied about certain details in her testimony to the court. Maybe she named the wrong man.

I quickly agreed to look into a DNA paternity test. Since I was the one doing the searching, I offered to pay for it.

We left the restaurant together and said our good-byes in the parking lot. Having brought a camera, I had Pat take pictures of Conrad and me standing together.

The photos would show us looking pretty happy. I wondered if we'd be that happy after our DNA test.

23

PATERNITY

As soon as we returned home from the meeting with Conrad, I called Jeanette. She was anxious to hear how it had gone and I happily filled her in. However, the possibility of Conrad's sterility concerned her.

Jeanette explained that I might be able to avoid the cost of a DNA test if we knew everyone's blood type. While that could not prove Conrad was my father, it might prove that he wasn't.

That's because certain blood type combinations are impossible. For example, my blood type is B. If Jackie happened to be A or O, my father would have to be B or AB, because my B had to have come from one of them.

First order of business: did Conrad know his blood type? If he did, we could try to find documentation of Jackie's blood type from the hospital records where she gave birth to my brother, Mike.

Since Conrad had been in the Army, his blood type would have been checked when he entered military service. In fact, it would be on his dog tags. I called him and explained what we were trying to do.

Unfortunately, Conrad did not know his blood type. And forty-five years after his discharge, he had no idea what happened to his dog tags.

On Monday, Conrad called his doctor's office and learned they had no record of his blood type. When he called me back with that news, I promised to set up the DNA paternity test.

I searched for a DNA testing lab and found one in Okemos, Michigan, a few miles east of Lansing. The location was perfect, roughly halfway between my home and Conrad's.

I called the lab and they answered all my questions. Yes, they could check paternity with just the child and the presumed father. They did not need to include the mother.

Good thing, I thought, since she had now been dead for forty-three years.

This was certainly the test we needed. When they told me the price, however, I nearly dropped the phone. Testing the two of us would cost six hundred dollars...and I had offered to pay for the test.

This may not seem like a great deal of money today, but in 1990, it was a king's ransom to me.

Pat and I talked it over and both of us reached the same conclusion: we had come so far that we wouldn't—no, couldn't—abandon our mission now. We would continue to forge ahead. By this time, I think we were both obsessed with learning the truth.

With Conrad's possible sterility hanging over the relationship, I could not simply assume that he was my father. Yet he was the man Jackie had identified as such. So I could not write him off, either.

After checking some possible dates with Conrad, I made the appointment for Tuesday, February 27, at 11 a.m. He and I met at the lab and they drew our blood. In about four weeks, they would mail the results to both of us. Four...long...agonizing...weeks.

After giving them our blood, Conrad and I found a nearby restaurant and had lunch together. It felt nice talking one-on-one with the man who might well be my biological father. We took our time and learned a lot more about each other.

For example, I discovered that Conrad had attended college twice, once in engineering and once in accounting. But he quit each time without getting a degree.

Since retiring, Conrad had owned a small apartment complex. A recent back injury now prevented him from using ladders and he had just sold the building.

After our leisurely lunch, we shook hands, got in our cars, and went our separate ways.

As expected, the next four weeks dragged. I wanted Conrad to be my birth father. I mean, I genuinely liked the guy. What's more, nearly nine years had passed since I began my search. Having already invested so much time and money in finding him, I dreaded the possibility of a negative result.

On March 24, 1990, Pat called me at my office. The day's mail had arrived and there was an envelope from the DNA lab. I told her not to open it.

I had waited so long for this moment that I had to read the results with my own eyes. Although I'm ordinarily a patient man, this day was an exception. I ducked out of work early and rushed home.

When I arrived, Pat handed me the envelope. My hands were almost trembling. This was the biggest moment of my search since meeting my brother.

Inside was a single sheet of paper with a table of unfamiliar numbers and letters. On a few rows, the word "Exclusion" appeared in the far right column. Below the table was a brief explanation of the results.

On one genetic marker, I did not have a particular value that Conrad must transmit to his children. On two other markers, a value that had to have come from my biological father was missing in Conrad's DNA.

In sum, the test proved—with absolute certainty—that Conrad was not my father.

While my search had gone pretty well to this point, inching closer and closer to the truth, this was a gigantic setback.

For nine years, I had been chasing the short Polish man that Jackie claimed was my father. Now that I had found him—and discovered he was a charming, intelligent gentleman—a DNA test proved he was not my father.

Tremendously deflated, I started to feel sorry for myself.

Then I remembered Conrad. He was counting on this test to give him the child he never thought he could have. Immediately, I got on the phone and called him. Yes, he had already opened the day's mail.

Even though Conrad was also disappointed, he was not nearly as surprised as I was. His conviction that he was sterile had grown stronger with every childless year. This clinched it.

I told Conrad I was sorry about the way this turned out and he said he was, too.

"You're a hell of a guy," he said.

I could already feel the loss deep in my gut. It was like—at long last—I had found my father. And then, just like that, I lost him again.

To his credit, Conrad helped me refocus on the search by making a suggestion. When he was dating Jackie, she had roomed with another girl at the boarding house in Plymouth. Conrad could not remember the girl's name, but he did recall that she had a Southern accent.

If I could find her, she might have been close enough to Jackie to know the name of my real biological father.

Thinking along the same lines, I asked Conrad if he could remember the name of anyone who worked with him and Jackie at Dann's Tavern. He could not. He did remember that the bar's owner was a guy in his thirties.

"Was that Dann?" I asked.

"No," Conrad said.

He was sure the owner was not named Dan or Dann. Whoever gave the bar its oddly spelled name was long gone by the time Conrad first walked in the door.

Before we hung up, Conrad and I agreed to stay in touch. But deep down, I think we both knew the basis for our relationship had evaporated. He was merely a man who had known and loved my mother for a short time during her short life. We were not related in any way.

24

COOKIE GIRL

Learning that Conrad could not be my father was a thunderous blow to my spirits. Pat tried to cheer me up with humor.

"At least you're not a Polack," she joked.

Not funny, I thought. Besides losing the man I was beginning to accept as my biological father, I had also lost 50 percent of my ethnicity. If I wasn't Polish, what was I? Maybe Dad was right all those years ago when he joked that I was a Heinz.

Another question began to nag at me. If Conrad was not my father, why on earth was his name in my adoption file? Obviously, the name came from Jackie. But why would she name the wrong man?

Pat and I talked it over and concluded there were only two basic answers: either Jackie made a mistake or she deliberately lied.

The first scenario suggested that Jackie was intimate with another man at roughly the same time as her relationship with Conrad. By the time she realized she was pregnant, many weeks would have passed and it may have been impossible for her to know which man was responsible. She had to guess and got it wrong.

The second scenario had Jackie falsely naming Conrad because the truth was more embarrassing. That would probably mean that my birth father was a married man.

Either of these possibilities could explain why Jackie never told Conrad about her pregnancy. She knew, or at least suspected, that he was not really the father of her second child.

My search had identified a number of men who Jackie dated in the two and a half years between her separation from Leonard and her death in the Jeep accident. As far as I knew, no one on my current list had been married at the time.

Thinking back, I had been able to eliminate a few of those men because they dated Jackie at the wrong time. Yet I also dropped others from consideration because they did not have Polish names.

Thankfully, I had saved all the notes from my countless phone calls, interviews, and other research. I would need to review everything with a fresh perspective.

Before I could do that, however, Pat reminded me of an incident from many years earlier that I had not even bothered to write down. As soon as she mentioned it, the memory came rushing back to me.

We had been shopping in a Grand Rapids mall when we stopped at a cookie store. A young girl behind the counter made of big deal of my "surprise" visit. Then realizing her mistake, she explained that I looked just like her boyfriend's father.

Naturally curious, I asked if the man was from the Detroit area and she said he was. This got me excited, so I asked if he was Polish. She laughed and said he was not. I then identified myself as adopted and explained that my unknown father was Polish. Convinced that the resemblance was merely a coincidence, we went on our way.

The missed opportunity of this chance encounter was now alarmingly obvious. What if her boyfriend's father was a brother of mine?

Since the boyfriend's family wasn't Polish, I did not bother to get the girl's name, her boyfriend's name, the family's nationality, or even a city within the vast region around Detroit.

That particular cookie store was no longer in business. What's more, Pat and I could not even agree on the year of that strange encounter.

I began to curse that "official" file in Lansing. Just like my two birth certificates, it was fraught with false information.

In all my years of searching for my birth families, the summer of 1990 was certainly the lowest point so far. The elimination of Conrad combined with the haunting memory of "Cookie Girl" left me dazed and a little depressed.

For the first time, I questioned if I should continue my search. Maybe I was not meant to know my birth father. Maybe fate was protecting me from something I was ill equipped to handle.

I felt drained and for the next several months I wallowed in that kind of negative thinking, turning my attention to family and work.

In October, I emerged from my funk when Jeanette suggested I write the Ingham County Probate Court to request a copy of my complete adoption file.

It was worth a shot, I reasoned. After years of back-and-forth correspondence, the judge and I were practically pen pals.

In my letter, I argued that keeping the file from me was no longer protecting anyone's privacy, since I knew the names of both "parents" named in the file.

Furthermore, my DNA paternity test with Conrad proved that half of the court's information was wrong. It gave me some small amount of satisfaction to tell him that and enclose a copy of the DNA report.

On December 5, the judge approved my request and a clerk asked me to submit $23.50 for photocopies. After spending six hundred dollars for the DNA paternity test, this was small change. I mailed a check.

The file arrived on December 13, 1990. It was a big day for me. I had done something that 99 percent of adoptees only dream about: I had acquired a complete copy of my legally sealed adoption file.

Initially, I was somewhat chagrined to see that most of the file—accounting for the majority of the copying cost—was the copious correspondence between the judge and me. I already had all that. The actual documents from 1946 formed a relatively small part of the file.

Still, I carefully pored through those records surrounding my birth and relinquishment. It was the story of my life, the basis for my existence. The fact that such records were forbidden fruit for adoptees made reading the file even more exhilarating.

My joy was tempered somewhat knowing that millions of other adoptees will never see their own files. For the sake of those receiving non-identifying information, I hoped other files were at least truthful.

Probably not, I thought. Surely, Jackie was not the only unwed mother to lie or otherwise misidentify a child's birth father.

Focusing on the task at hand, I compared the court documents with information I already had in my notes. There were a few key dates and addresses I lacked and some minor new details. I had hoped to find a clue hinting at the identity of my real birth father. Yet there was nothing to suggest anyone but Conrad.

Still, I did find two new items of interest.

When I learned earlier that Jackie was afraid her out-of-wedlock child might cost her custody of Michael, I had assumed it was Leonard about whom she was worried. Not so. It was Leonard's mother, Mrs. Bojanzyk, who was trying to get legal custody of her grandson.

The second piece of news made me smile. It was a social worker's statement that "Mrs. Hill and Jackie are fond of each other."

I remembered Mom's harsh comment about Jackie, during the one conversation we had about my adoption. It was nice to hear that even Mom liked her in 1946.

Following a seasonal pattern, my business workload dropped dramatically in the last two weeks of December 1990. I took some unused vacation time and stayed home to review my search records.

My best lead soon became apparent.

Carol Woods had learned Jackie's name from some relatives in her mother's family. Those same relatives had mentioned a rumor that someone in their family got Jackie pregnant.

Unfortunately, they had refused to reveal who it was. And I had not followed up, because the man was not Polish.

In the one conversation I'd had with Mom about my adoption, she insisted Carol's mother had checked out that rumor and determined it to be false. But with so many lies and cover-ups surrounding my birth, I decided to initiate my own investigation of that longstanding rumor.

25

RUMOR REVISITED

Nine years had passed since I spoke with Carol's distant cousins, Barb and Lorraine. Carol's great uncle, Bill French, had been their father. Although they willingly provided me with Jackie's name, they had balked when I asked about my birth father.

That's because a man in their family had been rumored to be the father of Jackie's baby. Decades after the fact, they had refused to reveal his name.

Since I was now forty-four and out of leads, I decided to call the sisters again. Lorraine's phone number was no longer in service, but Barb's number rang through.

Fortunately, Barb remembered me from our prior conversation. I shared that I had found the Polish man Jackie named as my father, but a DNA paternity test proved he was the wrong man.

Although she was still not ready to reveal the man's name, Barb was, nevertheless, sympathetic to my situation. As we talked, I could tell she was trying to walk a fine line between helping me and keeping a family secret.

Since Barb was willing to listen, I kept talking, reviewing all the reasons I wanted to identify my birth father. Then I wore her down some more by telling her about all the years I had wasted tracking the wrong man.

Her empathy growing, she revealed that the man was an uncle, married to one of her mother's sisters.

Thinking of the scenario where Jackie might lie to hide an affair with a married man, I asked if her uncle had been married at the time Jackie got pregnant.

"No," Barb said. "His fling with Jackie occurred before he met my aunt."

However, she continued, "When Jackie got pregnant there was a rampant rumor that he was the father. Everyone in my family just understood that it was his baby."

"Did your aunt ever hear that rumor?" I asked. Barb did not know. But she did worry about her aunt and uncle's reaction if someone were to ask them about it today.

Barb went on to tell me that her uncle had served in the Army during World War II. Just three years ago, he had retired after a successful career at Ford.

That would probably make him sixty-eight, I thought. Crunching the numbers in my head, I determined that he would have been about four years older than Jackie.

When I asked Barb to describe his appearance, she said he was a handsome man about five feet ten inches tall. He had two grown sons, both of whom were taller than he was.

Just as I was thinking that I now had enough clues to ferret out the man's name on my own, Barb's wall of secrecy broke down completely.

"I think you have a right to know your father," she said, pausing for a moment.

"His name is Roy Klann and he lives in Livonia. If you speak with him, please don't tell him you got his name from me."

Wow! I didn't expect that. Carefully, I added all this new information to my notes and confirmed the spelling of Roy's last name. I thanked Barb sincerely and ended the call.

I then dialed directory information for the Detroit area and got Roy's phone number and complete street address.

Next, I called Carol and shared what I had learned. She had heard of Roy, but at first, she could not remember where he fit in Barb's family. Then she recalled that he was married to a younger sister of Barb's mother. Unfortunately, she didn't know much more about him.

I then called Aunt Lynn and Conrad to see if the name Roy Klann was familiar. The name did not ring a bell with either one of them.

My final call was to Jeanette, my trusty search angel, who always knew the right thing to do. I explained that I had Roy's name, address, and phone number, but I didn't want to upset his wife or get either of them mad at Barb.

Jeanette promised to think it through and come up with a strategy for reaching Roy discreetly. Then Jeanette shared an unexpected piece of news.

While working on another adoption case, she was able to see what she described as my original birth record from the hospital. It was not a legal birth certificate like the other two I had. Jeanette would not reveal how she found it. So I accepted her vagueness about the source and just recorded the information she had found.

My original first and middle names, given to me by Jackie, were Gerald and Lee. On the paper that Jeanette saw, someone had crossed out "Gerald Lee" and replaced it with "Richard Harold."

I knew that "Lee" was Jackie's middle name and "Harold" was my adoptive father's first name. So the middle name transition from "Lee" to "Harold" made perfect sense. It was the first name transition that surprised me.

Mom had insisted that she and Dad named me "Richard" because it was simply a name they liked. I had doubted that story, wanting to believe that Jackie named me "Richard" after Leonard's kid brother. But these new facts shot down that speculation. Mom had told the truth about the origin of my name.

But why had Jackie chosen the name Gerald?

I had not run across that name in her family and I wondered if she might have named me after my biological father.

26

ROY

I rechecked all my records and the only man with a name close to Gerald was Jerry Jarskey, one of the men Jackie had dated. But according to an old city directory, his formal name was "Jarrold" with a "J" and not "Gerald" with a "G."

I tucked away the information on my original name, not knowing if it would ever prove to be useful or not. Then I turned my attention back to the best suspect I'd had since Conrad: Roy Klann.

Wanting desperately for all the pieces to fit, I wondered if Cookie Girl's boyfriend, whose father looked like me, could be a grandson of Roy Klann. If that were the case, there might be a young man named Klann living in the Grand Rapids area today.

Anxiously, I checked the local phone book for the name Klann and found a single listing. Without any plan at all, I dialed the number. As it was ringing, I decided to ask if he had ever dated a girl who worked at the now-closed cookie store in the mall.

A man answered who identified himself as a roommate. He said Klann was out but would return the following afternoon. I thanked him and hung up.

With time to think, I realized that an out-of-the-blue call from a complete stranger about one's dating history might be kind of alarming. Not wanting to upset anyone, I decided not to call again.

Still, my call wasn't wasted. I now knew that the Klann in Grand Rapids was single and lived with a roommate. That suggested he was young enough to be Cookie Girl's boyfriend.

Once again, pieces of my puzzle seemed to be falling into place. Even though I had to put my search on hold through the holiday season, I enjoyed the warm glow of optimism that had been missing since the paternity test with Conrad.

In mid January 1991, I called Jeanette only to learn that she was leaving for Las Vegas and would not return until late February. I was on my own for awhile.

Before contacting Roy, I figured it would be nice to know if I looked anything like him or his offspring. If one of his sons was, indeed, the father of Cookie Girl's boyfriend, the resemblance should be obvious.

On the first Tuesday in February, I took a half-day vacation and made another trip to Plymouth. My first stop was the historical museum that had the old Plymouth High School yearbooks. I didn't know if Roy went to the same school that Jackie had attended, but it was possible.

Checking the Plymouth yearbooks for the period did not yield any students named Klann. The city directories listed a Fred and Dorothy Klann in the Plymouth rural routes. I wondered if they might have been Roy's parents.

The area east of Plymouth, formerly Livonia Township, was now the city of Livonia. Since that was Roy's current residence, my next stop was the Livonia Civic Center Library.

If Roy had lived in Livonia when his sons were growing up, they might be in the Livonia high school yearbooks.

I learned that Livonia had two high schools in the late sixties and early seventies when Roy's sons would probably have been students. I checked Franklin High School first and did not find anyone named Klann.

Checking Bentley High School proved to be more productive. There was a Roy Klann in the class of 1967 and a Rod Klann four years behind him in 1971.

Roy and Rod? With such similar names, I thought, they had to be brothers, or at least cousins.

Both boys appeared to be slender in build. Roy (presumably Roy, Jr.) had light hair and a square jaw and looked nothing like me. Rod, on the other hand, at least had dark hair and a narrow chin. Yet even he did not jump off the page as my obvious double.

I had been hoping that the Roy Klann rumor and the Cookie-Girl story might merge in a son of Roy who looked just like me. But it was not to be.

Since I had the elder Roy's address and was already in Livonia, I drove by his house. The man had retired from Ford, so I was not surprised to see a Ford Taurus and a Ford Bronco in the driveway.

Not wanting to arouse suspicion, I kept going until I was out of sight. I waited about ten minutes and then made another pass from the opposite direction.

This time the Taurus was gone. I wondered if that was his wife's car and Roy might now be home alone. Would this be a good time to just show up at his door and introduce myself as Jackie's son?

Although I was sorely tempted, I remembered the rude and uncooperative response I got when I called Tom Martin. Not wanting to face that kind of rejection in person, I decided to take it slowly and wait for Jeanette to return from Las Vegas.

Having thought to bring my camera, I surreptitiously took a photo of Roy's house and then began the long drive back to Grand Rapids.

On the first Friday in March 1991, I was at work, but couldn't get my mind off Roy Klann and the fact that he might be my father. Giving in to my urges, I closed my office door and called Jeanette. Since I was more comfortable writing letters than making cold calls by phone, I suggested that I write Roy a letter and mark it "Personal and Confidential" to discourage his wife from opening it.

Jeanette did not like the letter idea, since he might choose not to respond. It was better, she thought, to catch him off guard by phone.

"OK," I said. "When can you call him?"

Since Roy's wife might answer, Jeanette decided that she could not make this call. A strange woman wanting to speak with her husband and refusing to disclose the subject would definitely be alarming.

"You should call him yourself," Jeanette said.

She suggested I start with my usual spiel about trying to contact people who knew my mother and see where the conversation went from there.

After ending the call with Jeanette, I waited for what seemed like an hour but was probably only several minutes. Then I cleared my throat and dialed the Klann number. A man answered and I confirmed it was Roy.

Our conversation turned out to be a brief one. The good news was that Roy did not ask me how I got his name or why I thought he knew my mother.

The bad news was that he claimed not to recognize Jackie's name. I tried another angle and asked if he knew Bill and Marion French. When he said he didn't know them either, I knew he was lying, because he and Bill had married sisters.

I apologized for bothering him and ended the conversation.

"Disappointed" is not an adequate description of how I felt. But at least the man had been cordial. It was nothing like the rude reception I got from Tom Martin.

When I reported the call to Jeanette, she said I might as well go ahead and send my letter. Having written many successful direct-mail letters in my career, I knew I could write a persuasive letter.

Without naming a source, my letter explained that I knew for certain he had dated my mother. I shared some of my history and my reasons for wanting to identify my father. I promised to keep our discussion confidential and I asked him to call me at his convenience. I enclosed my business card on which I had added my home phone number.

Adding the business card was a subtle way of assuring him that I was not some destitute street person looking for money.

Six days later our receptionist buzzed my office and asked if I could take a call from a Roy Klann. This was it, I thought, and I had her forward the call to my extension.

If I said my heart wasn't pounding as I heard Roy's voice on the other end, I'd be lying. He sounded friendly and apologized for not being more helpful when I called him the previous week. Admitting that he did know Jackie, he went on to explain how they met.

He was in the Army Air Corps serving in Texas and had just come home on furlough in December 1944. One of his first stops was a favorite watering hole, Dann's Tavern, where boys in the military rarely used their own money for drinks. It was there that he met Jackie.

I knew December was the month that Jackie had left Leonard and moved in with her mother near Dann's. So she must have just started working at the bar.

Roy was smitten with Jackie.

"She was one of the most attractive girls I ever met," he reflected.

He gave her a ride home from work one night, but he did not see her again until his next furlough in May 1945.

"She was a hard girl to get a date with, but I succeeded."

Ray then asked when I was born. I told him May 20, 1946, which suggested a conception date around August 20, 1945.

"It can't be me," Roy concluded. "I know I was in Texas on V-J Day, which was August 14. In fact, the May furlough was the last time I was in Michigan until November."

I had to admit that those dates eliminated him from consideration. He could have been lying, of course. But I didn't think so.

Roy told me he would be gone the following week on a trip. But if I wanted to meet with him in person, he could arrange something in April. He even offered to meet me halfway between Livonia and Grand Rapids.

I couldn't see any reason for us to meet. I felt he was being straight with me. Plus, he wouldn't know anything about Jackie's love life in the crucial August time period. So I thanked him for the offer and we ended the call.

Faced with the realization that I had drilled another dry well, my spirits sank again. I decided to take a break from my search.

Still, in the back of my head I had this vague feeling that I had missed something important.

27

GIRLFRIENDS

There's something magical about December. No matter when my search stalled out, it was most likely to restart in the weeks before or after Christmas.

The seasonal lessening of my business workload was sometimes a factor. But our Christmas card list now included my brother Mike, Aunt Lynn, Cousin Linda, my almost-father Conrad, and my grandfather Tony's widow, Harriet Hartzell.

Exchanging cards and letters with these people could not help but remind me of the unfinished search for my biological father.

December 1992 was a perfect example. I had not done a thing on my search since Roy Klann had eliminated himself twenty-one months earlier.

Suddenly, I remembered Conrad's comment that Jackie was close to a girl from the South who lived in the same rooming house. If I could find her, I thought, there was a good chance she would know the identity of my birth father.

In a moment of perfect hindsight, I thought back to all the interviews I did back in the eighties. I had only asked about Jackie's boyfriends. I now realized that I should have also been asking about her girlfriends.

Maybe it wasn't too late. There had to be people still living in the Detroit area who remembered Jackie. I reasoned that I might reach some of them through a classified ad in local newspapers.

Finding an inexpensive source on the Internet, I set up a toll-free phone number that rang into our home phone. Then I wrote the following ad and placed it in several small, local newspapers that covered Plymouth, Livonia, and Northville:

REMEMBER JACKIE HARTZELL BOJANZYK, Plymouth girl killed in 1947 Jeep accident? Her son, born 5-20-46, needs identity of biological father for medical reasons. Call days or evenings.

I also tried to place the ad in the *Detroit News* and the *Detroit Free Press*, but they would not run an ad with a last name other than my own. That restriction made no sense to me, but it was their policy.

My first caller was a woman named Kay. She remembered Jackie as a waitress at Cavalcade Inn and recalled that the bar's owner, Tom Martin, was the driver of the Jeep. She wondered if Tom might be my father.

She had no knowledge of a relationship between them. She just knew that Jackie had been in the Jeep with Tom, who had quite a reputation as a ladies' man. She also did not know anything about Jackie's personal life or any of her female friends.

I took down her comments and thanked her for calling. Once again, I shuddered at the thought of Tom Martin being my father. While driving drunk, he had killed a total of four people in two separate accidents.

On New Year's Day 1993, I received my second and last call in response to the ad. It was from a woman named Martha.

She had known Jackie and Jackie's sister, Joyce. In fact, she used to bowl with Jackie. She had met Jackie through a friend named Cordie who, like her, was from Tennessee. In fact, Cordie had been Jackie's roommate.

That's the one, I thought excitedly. Cordie must be the girl with the Southern accent who Conrad remembered as living in the boarding house with Jackie.

"Is Cordie still around?" I asked anxiously, almost holding my breath that the woman was still alive.

"I believe so," Martha said. "I have not talked to her in about three years, but she was still in the Detroit area at that time."

Martha promised to call the number she had for Cordie and get back to me, which she did in less than an hour. Cordie was still in the Detroit suburbs and was thrilled to hear that I had called.

According to Martha, Cordie knew all about Jackie's pregnancy and her long stay with my adoptive parents in Lansing. She also knew the identity of my biological father.

I had finally hit the mother lode. Cordie had been Jackie's best friend at the time of my conception and knew my whole story. I was thrilled beyond words.

Impulsively, I asked Martha if Pat and I could drive down and meet her and Cordie somewhere. She checked with Cordie, called right back, and said they would be happy to meet us. We set up a meeting at Cordie's home for the next day, which was a Saturday.

As Pat and I made the two-and-a-half-hour drive, we reflected on all the earlier trips I had made alone for research and all the trips we had made together to meet people.

With luck, I thought, we might soon be making another trip to meet my birth father.

There was also a certain irony that I could not escape: In a decade of searching, I had just now thought of using a newspaper ad to find people who knew Jackie. And I was in the advertising business!

Upon reaching Cordie's house, we received a warm, excited reception from both Cordie and Martha. Then we all sat down around Cordie's kitchen table and I brought out my pad of paper to take notes.

Cordie first met Jackie at Dann's Tavern, where they both worked as waitresses. She and Jackie became close friends and then roommates at the boarding house on Church Street in Plymouth.

Jackie and Cordie shared a number of girlfriends like Martha, Wanda, Marilee, Shirley, Betty, and a second Martha. Most of the girls were from the South. Wanda was the only other one who worked at Dann's.

Except for Cordie and the Martha sitting across from me, the others were all gone, either having died or moved out of state decades before.

Although the others may have heard or guessed about Jackie's pregnancy, Cordie felt she was the only one with whom Jackie shared her most personal feelings.

According to Cordie, all Jackie ever wanted was to marry and have children. But even though she loved her husband, Leonard, he had been so cruel to her that she had to leave him. Jackie also loved her son, Michael, and it broke her heart to give him up. But she had no way to support him.

When Jackie discovered she was pregnant again, she quit her job at Dann's and worked for a little while in a restaurant. Then she dropped out of sight.

Cordie believed she was the only friend who knew Jackie had gone to Lansing to live with people who were going to adopt her baby.

"She left the area in early January, right after the holidays," Cordie said. "Your parents supported Jackie for several months and paid all her medical bills."

Then, as if another memory had come flooding back, Cordie continued. "When Jackie came back in May, I asked her if she might try to get the baby back someday. She told me she would never do that because your parents had been so good to her."

When I heard that, my eyes started to water. Jackie's words made me proud of her and my adoptive parents. They had worked together to ensure that I would grow up with a family to love me.

Cordie went on to explain that the rooming house had filled up by the time Jackie returned and she could not get back in. So Jackie rented a room from a couple on Blunk Street in Plymouth.

The homeowner worked at Burroughs, as did Cordie by then. So Jackie soon got a job there, too. Then every weekday this man drove Jackie and himself to work, picking up Cordie along the way. Cordie could not remember the man's name, only that he had a wife and children.

"Jackie and I also worked off and on at Cavalcade Inn," Cordie continued. "A lot of my Southern friends hung out there. It was like a big family gathering."

That reminded me of Tom Martin.

"I hope you can assure me that Tom Martin was not my father," I pressed. Cordie and Martha both laughed. Cordie herself had dated Tom for awhile, but she assured me that Jackie never did.

"I spoke to Jackie the day she was killed," Cordie said. "She had eaten dinner at Barney's Grill, as she often did. She called me and wanted me to stop by Cavalcade Inn. She mentioned that her sister was in town and she was trying to find someone who would give Joyce a ride home."

Martha spoke up.

"I did hear," she said, "that Tom paid for the girls' funeral." Hmmm, I thought. That was the least he could do.

Cordie then surprised me by mentioning that she still visits Jackie's grave in Grand Lawn Cemetery occasionally. She rattled off the section, block, and grave numbers from memory.

They must have been incredibly close, I thought. Jackie has been dead for forty-six years.

I also thought, somewhat ashamed, that in all my trips to Detroit I had not even bothered to find the cemetery. That was odd, I thought. While some invisible force kept driving me to learn the details of Jackie's life, there was no pull to visit her grave. Maybe you have to know someone in life to attach any importance to his or her final resting place.

Our discussion so far had been informative and mesmerizing. Cordie's stories meshed well with what I already knew. But she still had not gotten around to answering my most important question: who was my birth father?

28

BOYFRIENDS

The suspense was killing me. Cordie had been Jackie's closest friend at the time of my conception. This woman was sitting on the answer to my biggest question and I was champing at the bit. I wanted to hear it now.

Looking directly at Cordie, I blurted out my question.

"Martha said you knew the identity of my biological father."

"Yes," she said. "Jackie told me who it was. I can see the man in my mind. He was short with light-colored hair, but for the life of me, I cannot remember his name. It's been so long."

Sheesh, another short guy, I thought. Jackie married Leonard and dated Conrad and both of them were short. Wasn't she attracted to anyone over five foot eight? Was she infatuated with Mickey Rooney types?

Cordie continued, "He was the only guy that Jackie ever saw steadily. He was a bartender at Dann's."

What? Steady boyfriend? A bartender? Noooooooooo! I screamed in my head. To my utter amazement, she was talking about Conrad.

Nearly overcome with disappointment, I asked in a somber tone, "Was his name Conrad?"

"That doesn't sound familiar," she replied.

Having brought my files with me, I dug out the photo of Conrad as a young man that he had given me at our first meeting.

"Is this the guy?"

"That's him!" Cordie exclaimed. "He was quiet and well mannered and everybody liked him. He and Jackie seemed quite compatible. But she was not ready to marry anyone and she warned me not to tell him she was pregnant."

"According to Conrad," I replied, "One of Jackie's girlfriends did tell him."

"It wasn't me," Cordie said with conviction. "I kept my mouth shut."

I did not doubt Cordie's statement. When Jackie dropped out of sight for five months, other people must have guessed she was pregnant. And lots of people must have known that she and Conrad had been a couple. Someone else had told him.

"Was Jackie certain it was his baby?" I asked soberly.

"She never expressed any doubts to me. Why do you ask?"

Letting out a sigh, I explained to Cordie and Martha that Jackie had indeed named Conrad in the adoption papers. But when I found Conrad, a DNA paternity test proved he could not possibly be my father.

"Well, I always thought it was him," Cordie replied, obviously perplexed.

I could see she was thinking, so I kept my mouth shut. Then Cordie broke the silence. "Now I remember...his name was Connie."

Pat spoke up. "That sounds like a nickname for Conrad."

I didn't share my thoughts, but Connie seemed like a strange name for a man. Then I remembered an old-time baseball player/manager called Connie Mack. So maybe it wasn't so odd back then.

"Jackie must have had sex with another man about the same time she was seeing Conrad, perhaps just before they started dating in late August," I said. "When she said he was my father, she was either mistaken or lying. If she lied, it might have been to cover up an affair with a married man."

"Jackie did not date married men," Cordie snapped defensively.

"I'm not saying she did," I answered. "I'm just describing the possibilities."

"Well, Jackie wasn't a slut," chimed in Martha.

"I'm not saying that, either," I responded. "I'm just reporting the fact that Conrad is not my father. It has to be some other man and I'm just trying to find out who it is."

Finally accepting the fact that Jackie had been wrong about Conrad being the father of her baby, Cordie and Martha tried to remember other men whom Jackie had dated. I also went through my notes and raised some possible candidates.

They confirmed that some of the men on my list, like Jerry Jarskey, had dated Jackie after I was born.

Other names I had, like Roy Klann, were unfamiliar to them. Either Jackie saw those men without their knowledge or these women had forgotten the names.

I even asked if Jackie knew anyone named Gerald, since that was the name she gave me when I was born. No luck.

"Jackie worked nights and I mostly worked days," explained Cordie. "So I have no way of knowing who she may have met at the bar. Most of the young guys from town were still in the service in 1945. Yet nearly all of them came by the bar whenever they were home on leave."

Cordie and Martha added some new names I had not heard before. My eyes reminded them of Arnold Ash and Harry Bowman. My smile made them think of Bud Murphy. They saw a man named Neil Curtiss in my expressions.

Although Jackie would have known all of these men, Cordie and Martha had no memories of her dating any of them. Besides resembling me in some way, the men had one other thing in common: they were all dead. Tracking them down for questioning was not an option.

On the other hand, Cordie did not think I looked like Tom Martin or Lester Barney.

According to Cordie and Martha, Jackie had been interested in some other guys whose names they could not remember. She went out once or twice with a guy from the Northville Bar. Although she liked him a lot, he was involved with someone else. Cordie also remembered that Jackie liked another guy from Northville who was in the Navy.

I then pointed out that the probable date of my conception would have been just a few days after V-J Day, when the Japanese surrendered to end World War II. That brought a smile to both their faces.

"Oh, boy," laughed Cordie. "That could explain why Jackie did not remember anyone but Conrad."

She continued, "Did you ever see that famous photo of the sailor kissing the girl on the street? I think it was in New York. Well, that's how it was here, too. The parties and drinking went on for days."

I asked if they remembered any specific V-J-Day celebrations involving Jackie. Cordie thought she and Jackie went together to the Box Bar in Ann Arbor one night. But other than that, she had no idea what Jackie was doing.

"We were all drinking like crazy and anything could have happened."

That's just great, I thought. My mother was already one of the most popular girls in the Plymouth-Livonia-Northville area. Now it looks like my father could have been a soldier or sailor in a drunken, one-night stand!

How could I discover the truth if Jackie didn't even know the truth?

Having exhausted the subject of Jackie's life in 1945, Pat and I thanked Cordie and Martha for taking the time to meet with us. Both women provided their phone numbers in case I had any further questions.

I had to admit that I did learn a lot on this trip and I was thrilled to meet some friends of Jackie face to face. Yet it seemed like the chances of ever learning the truth about my biological father had plunged to a new low.

What could I do next? What ground hadn't I already covered? Like many times before, it would be Jeanette, my search adviser from Adoptees Search for Knowledge, who suggested the critical next step.

29

SOCIAL INSECURITY

After returning home from our visit with Cordie and Martha, I got on the phone again. My first call was to Aunt Lynn. I wanted to see if she remembered these girlfriends of Jackie. She did remember Cordie but not Martha.

Next, I called Conrad. He did not remember Cordie's name, but he was certain I had found Jackie's roommate and closest friend. Hoping he could remember some other men that Jackie dated, I went through my latest notes and recited all the names I had just heard. He did not recognize any of them.

"It's just been too long for me to remember names," he sighed.

Since we last talked, however, Conrad had remembered a couple incidents about other men Jackie had dated.

First, he remembered that Jackie had gone out a couple times with the owner of Dann's Tavern. Conrad could not recall the guy's name, but on one occasion, he had borrowed Conrad's car to take Jackie out because his wife was using his.

That memory caught my attention, because it conflicted with Cordie's assertion that Jackie did not date married men.

In Conrad's second recollection, Jackie borrowed his car keys and disappeared one night when they were working together at Dann's. She returned with a man Conrad did not know and the two of them sat at the bar having drinks and acting a little too cozy for Conrad's comfort.

"Jackie and I dated steadily but not exclusively," Conrad explained. "She had never agreed to stop dating other men. But when she used my car to do it, I felt she was taking advantage of me. That's when I broke it off with her."

After finishing up with Conrad, I called Cordie and shared Conrad's new recollections. Jackie's use of the car surprised Cordie, because she had never seen her friend drive. But then, her date could have done the driving.

The idea of Jackie with the owner of Dann's Tavern was a complete shock. Besides being married, the man was at least ten years older than Jackie. Cordie could not recall his name either. Dann had been a prior owner.

Before I could ask, Cordie remarked that I did not look like the bar's owner. She went on to say that he had moved to Texas and bought another bar. She also remembered hearing that he had died.

That's wonderful, I thought sarcastically, another deceased suspect.

Cordie went on. After thinking about her list of men who had resembled me in some way, she remembered that Jackie had indeed dated Bud Murphy. He was divorced at the time and lived in an apartment over Ellis Restaurant.

If Jackie was not above dating married men, Cordie added, then Harry Bowman, whose eyes looked like mine, would have been a candidate. He was a superintendent at Wall Wire.

Hmmmm, I thought. Jackie had falsely described Conrad as a coworker at Wall Wire. Maybe she was telling half the truth. Maybe Harry Bowman was my biological father and she told everyone it was Conrad to avoid revealing an affair with a married man.

The next day, I called Jeanette and brought her up to date. Jeanette was old enough to remember big-time partying on V-J Day. If that historical event had brought my biological parents together for a single, alcohol-fueled union, my father was unlikely to have known that he helped create a child.

And my chances of discovering his identity would be near zero.

Jeanette did her best to keep me motivated. As a next step, she suggested I write the Social Security Administration for Jackie's earnings record for 1945 through 1947. That would list all the places she worked and might tell us the name of the man who owned Dann's Tavern.

Following Jeanette's instructions, I found Jackie's Social Security number on her death certificate and completed the form to request her detailed Social Security earnings information.

I enclosed a copy of the death certificate to prove she was deceased. Needing to prove my relationship to the deceased, I included a copy of my original birth certificate that listed Jackie and husband, Leonard Bojanzyk, as my parents. Jeanette warned me not to suggest adoption in any way, so I signed my name as Richard Bojanzyk.

In the section asking why I needed this information, I wrote the following:

"I am writing a family history and need to know places where my mother worked before she died in 1947."

In April 1993, returning home from a family vacation, I picked up a big pile of mail that had been held at the Post Office. Within the stack was an envelope from Social Security.

Inside was a two-page "Itemized Statement of Earnings." The report summarized Jackie's earnings—by quarter—for each employer. By tracking the ebb and flow of her earnings and comparing them with what I already knew, I was able to piece together her employment history.

Jackie's first employer, right after she left Leonard, was Douglas S. Richards, DBA Dannie Tavern. That had to be Dann's Tavern. And now I had the name of the owner with whom Jackie had gone out a couple times.

Based on the dollar figures, Jackie worked at Dann's full-time at first. By the second quarter of 1945, her earnings at the bar had dropped dramatically and the majority of her earnings were from Wall Wire.

There were no reported earnings from Dann's after the second quarter. That made sense, because Jackie's waitressing dropped to part time after getting the Wall Wire job. Plus, Cordie had told me that bars routinely paid their part-time staff in cash. That would also explain why Cavalcade Inn, where Jackie worked part-time after my birth, was completely missing from the report.

One employer that surprised me was Lingeman Products. I knew it was a small manufacturing plant next to Cavalcade Inn because Earl Smith—the millionaire wife-killer—told me that he and Jackie's sister, Joyce, had both worked there for awhile.

Earl had not mentioned Jackie working there, but Social Security reported a small amount of earnings during the third quarter of 1945. That July-to-September quarter covered the time when Jackie got pregnant. Did Earl forget to mention Jackie's employment at Lingeman or was he hiding something?

My God, I thought, the possibilities just keep growing!

In the last quarter of 1945, Jackie earned small amounts from Livonia Grill, Ellis Restaurant, and the D&C dime store. Cordie had said that Jackie left Dann's after learning she was pregnant and worked in a restaurant. Presumably, she was uncomfortable working with Conrad, because she did not want him to push her into marriage.

Ellis Restaurant caught my eye because Cordie had said Bud Murphy had an apartment over that business. Was that just a coincidence or did it mean something?

As expected, Jackie had no reported earnings from January to May 1946 when she lived in Lansing with my adoptive parents.

When she returned from Lansing, her first two jobs were at Daisy Manufacturing Company and Al's Italian Restaurant. By October 1946, she was working at Burroughs, where she continued working until her death in June 1947.

I called Cordie the next day. She confirmed that Doug Richards was indeed the name of the man who owned Dann's Tavern. In spite of Conrad's recollection, Cordie still doubted that Jackie would have dated him. And knowing his name didn't help much, because he had already passed away.

Cordie knew all the businesses on Jackie's earnings report. But she only remembered Jackie working at a few of them. She told me that

Wall Wire made bombsights during the war and Daisy Manufacturing made BB guns.

Next, I called Martha. The name Doug Richards meant nothing to her, but unlike Cordie, she never worked at Dann's Tavern. She also remembered many of the other businesses on Jackie's employment list. She and Cordie also had worked at Wall Wire for awhile before Jackie did.

Then Martha surprised me with her next comment. Unlike Cordie, she believed that a relationship between Jackie and Tom Martin was possible.

"I keep recalling some vague memory of the two of them together," she said. "I can't be sure, but I would not rule it out. Plus, you and Tom have the same dark, nearly black hair."

When I hung up the phone, I felt a little discouraged. I thought Cordie had eliminated Tom Martin as a suspect, but now I couldn't even be sure of that.

Well, I thought. What now?

For the first time since beginning my search some twelve years earlier, I could not answer that question. I was stumped. Baffled. Flummoxed.

I now knew that Conrad had been Jackie's only steady date. He was also the only man that I knew for sure had been intimate with her. And he was the only man I could eliminate with certainty because of DNA testing. So I didn't have any solid leads.

I had one list of men who had gone out with my mother for relatively brief periods but did not look like me. Then I had another list of men who were simply in the community and looked a little like me. Not exactly a lot to go on.

Any one of these guys could have been my birth father. But nothing made any one candidate stand out from the rest. Furthermore, I couldn't interview any of these men, since all were either dead or old enough to be retired in some unknown location.

Even worse, the possibilities were not limited to either list of known suspects. As a pretty girl waitressing in a bar, Jackie could have met hundreds of men, including countless randy young soldiers and sailors home on leave from the war.

Jackie did not have a car. How many men, like Roy Klann, had given her a ride back to her Plymouth rooming house after work?

Around the time of my conception, Jackie also worked at two manufacturing plants: Wall Wire and Lingeman Products. She could have gotten involved with a supervisor or coworker at either plant.

Then there was the V-J Day scenario. The end of that long, dreadful war had people partying from coast to coast. Under the influence of intense joy and lots of alcohol, thousands of young women were thanking soldiers in an extremely personal way for their service to our country.

If Jackie was among them—and at this point, that was sounding like a real possibility—I might never be able to identify my birth father.

My calls to Cordie and Martha, on April 12, 1993, were the final entries in my notes from the 1990s. I never spoke or even thought the words "quit" or "give up." Yet it would be many years before I restarted my search.

30

TRANSITIONS

In 1994, Mom was diagnosed with ovarian cancer. Her oncologist performed the recommended surgery. But by February 1995, the cancer had spread, leaving her with an estimated six months to live.

Mom wanted to stay in her Ionia apartment. But a fire in a neighbor's unit soon made that impossible. With her apartment condemned and most of her possessions ruined by smoke and water damage, Mom moved in with us.

Having lived alone since Dad's stroke eighteen years earlier, Mom cherished her independence. In spite of deteriorating health, she demanded that we find her a new apartment. Reluctantly, we found and furnished one in a senior citizen complex about ten minutes from our home.

She stuck it out for three days.

The turning point was the second night, when Mom discovered that she no longer had the strength to climb into bed unassisted. Finally facing the inevitability of her situation, she agreed to enter a local hospice facility.

The hospice home was about ten minutes from my office and once again, I found myself having regular lunches with a parent whose life was fading away. In this case, Mom's mind and vision were still sharp and we often played Tonk or Cribbage, her favorite card games.

Remembering how relieved Dad was after talking about my adoption, I hoped Mom would experience a similar catharsis. The adoption was no longer a secret, of course. But she and I had never re-opened the subject in the thirteen years since my "confession" letter triggered that one conversation.

Several times, I came close to bringing it up. I wanted to tell her again that knowing I was adopted had done nothing to diminish her place in my life. She had been and would always be my real mother.

Yet I also knew how hard she had tried to convince me and most of the world that she was my only mother. Fearing that forcing open that closet would cause her pain, I said nothing and waited. I kept hoping she would initiate the conversation as Dad had done.

August 1995 arrived, the final month of her doctor's six-month projection. One day, after sitting up and soundly beating me in a game of Tonk, Mom lay back down with a satisfied look on her face. A couple of hours later, the hospice nurse called my office to report that Mom had lost consciousness. I returned to her room and—just as I had with Dad—stayed with her until she stopped breathing.

In addition to the usual sadness when a parent dies, I felt an extra loss. In all my adult years, Mom and I had only discussed my adoption that one time—and it was by telephone. Ever since our one conversation, we had both ignored the elephant in the room.

Was I right to let her die with the subject caught in my throat? Should I have been the one to break the silence? I did not know the answer.

After Mom's death, a cousin recalled an incident from when she was pregnant. She happened to run into my mother in a downtown store. As they discussed my cousin's pregnancy, Mom chimed in with tales of her own pregnancy, including memories of morning sickness!

Aware that I was adopted, my cousin knew this was a fantasy. But she chose not to challenge Mom's story.

Neither female nor a psychologist, I cannot explain Mom's deep-seated need to have borne her own child. But my cousin's story made me feel a little better about not forcing open the subject.

While my parents were alive, I had always respected their privacy, even after beginning my search. With both of them gone, however, it was now my responsibility to search through Mom's papers for legal documents and unpaid bills.

Naturally, I kept my eyes open for documents or correspondence relating to my adoption. I found nothing. Absolutely nothing. The paper trail had been wiped clean.

I remembered my aunt's remark about my grandmother burning papers and letters pertaining to my adoption. Letters, I suddenly thought. Who would have written letters about me?

My birth mother, Jackie, had lived with my adoptive parents for five months before I was born. It was not unreasonable to think she may have written to them in the thirteen months between my birth and her death. Such letters would have been precious to me now. But if such correspondence ever existed, it was long gone.

Ten months after Mom's death, Mark and Catherine graduated from high school. Jenny had preceded them in 1991. Knowing families who had frequently uprooted their children from schools and friends, Pat and I had been determined not to do that. By remaining in the same suburb for twenty-one years, all three of our children had stayed in the same school district from pre-school through high school graduation.

By the fall of 1996, however, we were empty nesters. No longer constrained by school district boundaries, I fulfilled a lifelong dream and we bought a home on a lake. The location was twelve miles from my office, the same distance as our prior home. Yet with less traffic in that part of the county, I cut ten minutes each way from my daily commute. I was thrilled.

By the time of this move, the search for my birth father had been stuck on life's back burner for nearly four years. It would remain there for another decade.

During this long hiatus, some of the wonderful people I encountered in searching for my roots passed away. Harriet Hartzell, my grandfather Tony's second wife and a fascinating pen pal, died in 1993. Conrad Perzyk, the Polish man my birthmother incorrectly named as my father, died in 1998.

My brother, Mike, sacrificed his bachelorhood to get married again. In 1999, he and his new wife took advantage of early retirement offers and relocated from the Detroit area to Tennessee. They built a new home—where else?—on a golf course.

Over the years, Mike and I had grown closer emotionally but were now much farther apart geographically. While personal visits became far less frequent, they now lasted one to three days. In good weather, we always included a round of golf.

I continued to play two or three times a year. Although I still wasn't breaking a hundred, I did occasionally get through eighteen holes with only one ball.

My career was going well. The ad agency I worked for had prospered and, at its peak, employed about fifty people. Then in 2001, we sold our employee-owned company to an out-of-state holding company.

When my employment agreement expired in the summer of 2004, I jumped eagerly into semi-retirement. Working part-time from home, I cut my workweek in half. Instead of working fifty to sixty hours a week, the new normal became twenty-five to thirty hours a week.

Instead of limiting myself to six or seven hours of sleep a night, I shut off my alarm clock and started waking up naturally after eight hours or so. At fifty-eight years old, my body had already been telling me that exercise was no longer optional. So I started working out more consistently at our health club three afternoons a week.

Within months, the combination of more sleep, more exercise, and less stress was making a new man of me. I felt better than I had in at least ten years.

My work-from-home existence did have drawbacks. As expected, I was earning a lot less money. What's more, I missed the daily interaction with longtime coworkers.

For awhile, I returned to my old workplace for brief visits. But it soon became clear that Pat and I needed to rebuild our social life in new directions not centered on my former employer.

One of those directions involved high school classmates.

During that first summer of self-employment, Pat and I attended my fortieth high school reunion in Ionia. Now that most of my classmates were empty nesters like us, talk of seeing each other between reunions was more realistic.

Pat and I began getting together periodically with some of my old classmates. We started out meeting in restaurants but gradually began to gather in each other's homes. While most of us lived somewhere in the Grand Rapids-to-Lansing corridor, which included Ionia, many of our gatherings were timed to include out-of-state classmates coming home to visit family.

In early December of 2006, we were meeting at the home of Joe Stewart, a classmate who still lived north of Ionia. We were enjoying dinner in his dining room when I happened to overhear a comment that would rekindle the search for my birth father.

31

INSPIRATION

With twelve of us seated around Joe Stewart's long dining room table, I was hearing several discussions at once. Yet through all the hubbub, one conversation reached out and grabbed me by the ears.

Joe was telling someone about a DNA test that helped people trace their family trees. Joe had ordered the test online and was hoping to trace his Stewart line further back in time.

The search for my birth father had been on hold for nearly fourteen years. I could not even remember the last time I had thought about it. Yet my mind latched onto this discussion and blocked out everything else.

Joe explained that this genetic test measured certain markers on a man's Y chromosome. These markers generally pass on unchanged from father to son, generation after generation. Since these men usually have the same surname, the test is a great tool for genealogists.

If another Stewart in the test company's database is a close match to Joe, he and that person would know for sure that they shared a common ancestor. Since people who match can e-mail each other, Joe would be able to work with that match to identify their common ancestor and expand their shared family tree.

In a flash of inspiration, I saw how that test could also be a great tool for adopted men like me. If I took the test and matched someone, he would be a biological relative from my birth father's family. Since our paternal lines had to intersect at a common male ancestor, he and my birth father should have the same last name.

If I were to take the test and match a Smith, for example, I would know that my birth father had been a Smith.

I told Joe that I wanted to know more and he promised to e-mail a link to the company's web site.

As I was explaining my idea to Pat on the drive home, I realized how fitting it was that I had gotten this DNA tip from Joe. He and I had first learned about DNA from our tenth-grade biology teacher, Mrs. Stewart, who happened to be Joe's mother!

She had been the one who explained away the eye-color discrepancy between my adoptive parents and me.

The next day, Joe e-mailed the link to me, as promised. The name of the DNA testing company was Family Tree DNA. I went to its web site and read about the new science that they called genetic genealogy.

As I thought more about the Y-DNA test, I realized that my plan might not be foolproof. What if my birth father was also adopted? Or what if his father was adopted? For my DNA match to have my biological surname, all of the men in his paternal line and mine had to use the same surname back to the common ancestor.

Family Tree DNA offered several options for its Y-DNA test. The least expensive one looked at twelve DNA markers. Tests for twenty-five, thirty-seven, and sixty-seven markers were available at higher prices.

Not yet understanding what extra markers could do for me, and trying to be conservative in my spending, I ordered a twelve-marker test.

DNA testing had advanced a lot since Conrad and I had met at the lab sixteen years earlier to have our blood drawn. The home test kit I received in the mail was simple and painless to use.

Following instructions, I used the swabs they provided to lightly scrape some cells from inside my cheeks. I then completed the paperwork and placed everything in the pre-addressed return envelope.

After dropping the envelope in the mail a couple days after Christmas, all I had to do was wait.

In late January 2007, I received my results in the mail. A certificate listed my values, technically called "alleles," for each of the twelve markers tested. For example, at marker DYS 393 my value was thirteen. At DYS 390, it was twenty-four, and so on.

These marker values can mutate over time. But such mutations occur so slowly that my biological father, grandfather, and their recent paternal-line ancestors almost certainly had the same values as I did at all twelve markers.

More exciting than the actual numbers was a password the company sent for my personal account at the Family Tree DNA web site. Using my kit number and password, I could now log in and see if I had any Y-DNA matches with other men in the database.

Anxiously, I went to my computer and accessed my account. Looking at a menu of choices, I selected Y-DNA Matches. A list of forty-two names and e-mail addresses appeared on the screen. To my amazement, every one of these men had exactly the same twelve-marker results as I did.

I scanned the surnames to see if any one name showed up multiple times. But each of my forty-two matches had a different surname. That was not what I expected at all!

Wondering if I could cull the list by geography, I e-mailed a few of the matches to ask if their ancestors had ever lived in Michigan. All replied "no" and a few went on to share details of their ancestral trees.

Fortunately, one respondent took the time to explain that our values for the first twelve markers were quite common among people of Western European heritage. That's why I had so many matches.

I would see a lot of irrelevant surnames because most twelve-marker matches resulted from common ancestors who lived many hundreds of years ago.

Given that much time, the odds increased that one line or the other would include a name change, an informal adoption, or a child secretly fathered by someone other than his mother's husband. As a result, the current surname in that line was out of sync with the true biological relationships tracked by the Y-DNA test.

Furthermore, some of the common ancestors from a twelve-marker match would be so far back in time that people were not yet using surnames. A man known as "John the baker," for example, had not yet adopted the name "John Baker."

To determine which matches had common ancestors from more recent times, I needed to test additional markers. He recommended an upgrade to thirty-seven markers.

After reading his message, I logged into my account at Family Tree DNA and ordered the upgrade. Since they already had my DNA, I did not need to submit another sample.

Around the first of March, I received an e-mail that my additional markers were ready for me to view online. Checking my account, I saw that only one of my forty-two matches at the twelve-marker level was still a match at a higher level. One man, who had tested twenty-five markers, matched me perfectly on all twenty-five.

His name was W. Wiley Richards.

Now I was excited. Could my birth father have been a Richards? I searched my memory but came up blank. Almost fourteen years had passed since I last looked at my search notes. I would have to dig them out to see if my birth mother, Jackie, had been around any men with that surname.

The following Sunday, I went to the basement and found the large, plastic file box where all my search notes and documents had lain untouched since we moved to the lake house. I brought the box upstairs and stacked the contents on the table next to my favorite chair. The pile of notebooks, documents, photos, and loose notes was nearly eighteen inches thick.

This could take awhile, I thought, settling in for the afternoon. But I was wrong. In less than a minute Pat heard me exclaim in a loud voice:

"I found him."

"What do you mean?" Pat looked up from the book she was reading.

"My birth father," I responded. "I finally know who he was."

32

HITTERS

With everything stacked on the table, the most recent document, Jackie's Social Security earnings record, waited for me on top of the pile. As soon as I picked it up and saw Dann's Tavern, the name of the owner jumped out at me: Douglas S. Richards.

Memories from my search came flooding back. Conrad Perzyk, who Jackie misnamed as my father, had been a bartender at Dann's when Jackie worked there as a waitress. He once told me the bar owner had gone out with Jackie.

That man was Doug Richards. And now my Y-chromosome was a perfect match to a man whose surname was Richards.

Coincidence? I didn't think so. My gut said Doug Richards was my biological father.

For the rest of the day, I dug through the pile—re-reading my notes from when I met Conrad and found Jackie's girlfriend, Cordie. I pulled together everything I had on Doug Richards.

He was at least ten years older than Jackie…and married. While an affair with a married man was not my dream story, I was excited to have a solid lead consistent with my DNA test results.

According to Cordie, Doug did not look like me. That, too, was disappointing. Since eliminating short, light-haired Conrad from consideration, I had again envisioned my birth father as a tall man with dark hair.

Cordie had told me that Doug moved to Texas and bought another bar. She also mentioned that he had died. If he was my father, I would once again be too late to meet my biological parent.

When the search for my birth father had gone cold fourteen years earlier, it was because I'd had too many suspects. Nothing made one stand out from the rest. Now my Y-DNA test had painted a bulls-eye on the name Doug Richards. I had a single candidate on whom to focus my sights.

Having gone down the wrong path with Conrad and others, I wasn't about to anoint Doug Richards just yet. The logic seemed right, but this could prove to be one of those situations where two and two did not make four.

Somehow, I had to prove or disprove that Doug Richards was the right man. I had no idea how to do that. But I felt confident I would figure it out.

The first step, I reasoned, was to contact my Y-DNA match through e-mail. Maybe he was in Michigan or Texas and could identify the branch of his family that included Doug.

I sent an e-mail to W. Wiley Richards, referring to our twenty-five-marker Y-DNA match at Family Tree DNA. I told him I lived in Michigan and asked him where he lived and where his ancestors had lived.

Wiley wrote back that he lived in Florida and his family had been in the state since his great-grandfather was born there in 1827. The most distant paternal ancestor he could trace with certainty was his great-great-grandfather, who was born in Franklin County, North Carolina in 1796. As far as Wiley knew, no one in his family had ever lived outside the Southeastern states.

Once again, my hope for a quick, easy solution did not pan out. Wiley's known family tree did not lead directly to Doug. Our common ancestor must have lived farther back in time than Wiley could trace.

My next thought was to re-contact Jackie's girlfriend, Cordie. If she knew more details about Doug Richards and his family, maybe I could trace his descendants.

I looked up Cordie's phone number in my notes, substituted the new suburban Detroit area code, and dialed. Would she still be alive? Would she remember me? When Cordie answered, I discovered the answer to both questions was yes.

Briefly, I filled her in on the Y-DNA test and my match to a man named Richards in Florida. I then reminded her that the only Richards on my long list of suspects had been Doug Richards, the owner of Dann's Tavern.

Cordie had not wanted to believe that Jackie was involved with a married man. But she had no trouble believing that Doug would have been interested in a young woman as beautiful as Jackie was.

"When did Doug move to Texas?" I asked.

"It was still in the forties," answered Cordie. "I remember hearing that he had a really big bar out there."

Cordie could not remember why Doug chose Texas or to what part of the state he had moved. But she did remember hearing about his death many years later.

"When did he die?" I asked.

Cordie had to reflect on that awhile, trying to remember what was happening in her own life when she heard the news.

"It would have been in the eighties," she concluded.

When I asked her about Doug's family, Cordie could not remember much. She had met his wife at the bar, but could not recall if they had children or not.

"He did have a brother, Jack," she remembered. "Jack owned another tavern on Joy Road called the Joy Bar."

"Everybody knew Doug and Jack," she continued. "I think one of them built a third bar called the Oasis that later became the Good Time Bar."

Cordie knew nothing about Jack's family and did not know where either of the brothers had lived.

"One of the brothers was into horse racing," she added. "I can't remember which one, but he owned quite a few race horses."

Thinking I might check the race tracks, I asked if the horses were thoroughbreds or trotters. Cordie couldn't remember.

Once I had tapped all her memories of Doug and his family, I thanked her again and ended the call.

I was feeling pretty confident that I could trace the family. Doug and his brother, Jack, were both prominent businessmen in the Livonia area. I had the names of three bars they were involved in: Dann's Tavern, the Joy Bar, and the Oasis. Plus, one of them owned race horses. There had to be a paper trail somewhere.

The problem, I realized, was that six decades had passed since my birth. Could I pick up a trail that cold? And would it lead me to family members living today?

Since I worked for myself now, it was a lot easier to take time off during the week when libraries and historical museums were sure to be open. On a Friday morning in March, I drove to Livonia.

Expecting this to be a challenging search of historical records, I stopped in Lansing to pick up an expert assistant: my cousin, Kathy. Four years younger than I was, Kathy had become the first genealogist in my adoptive mother's family. With two of us looking through the records, I figured we could cover more ground.

Kathy and I drove by the site of Dann's Tavern at the southwest corner of Plymouth and Stark. There wasn't even a building there. It was just a used car lot.

Our stops at Civic Center Library and Greenmead Historical Museum were not especially productive. Since Livonia did not even become a city until 1950, there were no old city directories like the ones that had proved so useful in Lansing and Plymouth.

We did find some old phone books. In the 1945 directory, I found a small Yellow Pages ad for Dann's Tavern that included the name "Doug Richards." I photocopied the page.

Cordie had told me that one of the Richards brothers built a bar called the Oasis that later became the Good Time Bar. That bar was no longer in business, but I learned there was still a bar in the same building. The new name was Hitters.

That sounded like a sports bar to me. We had to eat lunch somewhere. Why not eat at Hitters? It would be cool to eat in a building with historical connections to my birth father's family.

My son, Mark, lived in the Detroit area and coincidentally was working in Livonia that week. So I invited him to meet Kathy and me for lunch at Hitters. I gave him the address.

Hitters was also on Plymouth Road, just a couple of blocks west of the Dann's Tavern site. A huge Ford factory loomed across the street. The bar was smaller than I expected with the entrance in the rear.

The place was dimly lit, a bit smoky, and smelled of stale beer. Kathy and I chose a clean table near the door so we could watch for Mark. As my eyes adjusted to the light, I could see that the clientele was totally blue collar and 100 percent male. Kathy was the only female customer in the place.

Although there was a TV near the bar, this was definitely not what I knew as a sports bar.

Our table was one of those high ones with the long-legged chairs. Like magic, a waitress appeared out of the haze. She had long blonde hair and a body that screamed surgical enhancement. Dressed in skin-tight short shorts and a bikini top, she leaned in to take our order.

Just then, as Kathy and I were struggling to project an air of normalcy, Mark walked in.

Taking in the atmosphere of the place, he saw me, my conservatively dressed cousin, and our scantily clad waitress engaged in conversation. Sensing the incongruity of the whole scene, Mark broke into a huge grin.

He then joined us and we ordered some burgers that turned out to be pretty good. After lunch, Kathy and I said good-bye to Mark in the parking lot and proceeded to our next stop.

The morning's research had identified the racetracks around Livonia. The Detroit Race Course had been a big deal for awhile; but racing there had ended in 1998. Now the only track still active was Northville Downs. We stopped by and could see they did harness racing. On a weekday afternoon in March, not much was going on.

I found a small building that served as the track's office and went inside. A young girl in her twenties was the only one there. I asked if she knew anyone who had been around the track for fifty years or more. She said she could think of a couple men, but they were not there that day.

I wrote out the names "Doug Richards" and "Jack Richards" on a piece of paper. Then I added my name and phone number below. I asked her to see if anyone remembered a horse owner by either of those names. If anyone did, would she ask him to call me?

The girl said she would do it. Maybe she did, maybe she didn't. Whatever the case, no one ever called.

Of all my research trips to the Detroit area, this was one of the least productive. Yet it was clearly the most memorable. Whenever I see Kathy at a family gathering, she always mentions our infamous lunch at Hitters.

33

ONLINE ASSISTANCE

In March 2007, I had a resource that was unavailable in the early years of my search: the Internet. Someone at the Livonia library suggested I try FamilySearch.org, a web site maintained by the Mormon Church.

Returning home from Livonia, I got on my computer, went to the site and filled out a search form. I entered Doug Richards and specified a death year of 1985 plus or minus five years in the state of Texas. This brought up the Social Security Death Index where only one record matched my query.

That record was for a Douglas Richards born in 1913 with a Social Security number issued in Michigan. He died in April 1986 and his last residence was Hillsboro, Texas.

This seemed like a perfect fit. He was thirteen years older than Jackie, had lived in Michigan, and died in Texas in the eighties as Cordie had remembered.

I then searched for "Hillsboro newspaper" and found the site of the *Hillsboro Reporter*. I called and asked how to find old obituaries. They told me that back issues were on microfilm and kept at the city library.

Calling the library, I learned that the staff would not search microfilm for me, but some volunteer genealogists probably would. I submitted a search request with Doug's name and the month and year of his death.

A couple days later, I received an e-mail with an obituary attached. The top line read Douglas S. Richards, Sr.

Noticing that the middle initial "S" was consistent with Doug's name on Jackie's Social Security record, I read every word with interest.

This Doug Richards was born in Texas and had lived in Michigan for ten years. Survivors included his widow, a son and daughter, and two brothers: Vernie in Michigan and Joe in Texas.

Some of the details, however, did not fit my expectations. He was listed as a retired rancher, not a bar owner, and he had stayed married to the same woman for fifty years. Would the Doug Richards that Cordie remembered have been able to do that?

Furthermore, there was no mention of a brother named John, which I assumed was Jack's real name.

Someone told me that the Social Security Death Index was only partially complete. It depended on survivors reporting the information to Social Security. Perhaps I had found the wrong Doug Richards.

Just in case it was the right family, I searched the online telephone directory for a Vernie Richards in Michigan, but did not find anyone. That did not surprise me. It was now ninety-four years after Doug's birth. His brothers might not be alive, either.

A search for "Livonia genealogy" led me to the Western Wayne County Genealogical Society. I submitted an e-mail inquiry with what I knew about Doug and Jack Richards. The organization's secretary responded with a number of search tips and promised to ask members with e-mail addresses if they knew of these men.

Within a couple days, I received an e-mail from a genealogist named John. He remembered a Vernie Richards from the Joy Bar who had been an instructor at the Henry Ford Trade School in Dearborn.

Continuing the e-mail exchange with John, I learned that Vernie and his wife were deceased, but they had a daughter, Gerry, who lived in a small town west of Detroit. Fortunately, he knew her married name.

Searching the online phone directory for that area, I found one listing for her last name and dialed the number. The man who answered told me Gerry was his cousin's wife, but he would not give out her number because it was unlisted.

Telling him that I wanted to discuss a family history matter, I asked if he would call her and relay my name and phone number. He agreed to do that and, later that same day, my phone rang.

The caller was Gerry, who asked politely how she could help me. I told her I was trying to find the family of Doug Richards, who had owned Dann's Tavern in the 1940s. She confirmed that Doug had been her uncle and that her father, Vernie, had owned the Joy Bar.

"I thought the owner of the Joy Bar was Jack Richards," I said, somewhat puzzled.

"My father's name was Vernie Fletcher Richards," she explained. "But a lot of people called him Jack. I have no idea where he got that nickname."

Gerry went on to tell me that the Richards family was from Texas and her father had four brothers and three sisters. Vernie was the oldest boy and came to Michigan to work for Ford, eventually becoming a teacher at the Henry Ford Trade School. Some of the other brothers followed him here.

"Which brother raced horses?" I asked.

"That was my dad," Gerry replied. "I don't think Uncle Doc ever got into racing."

"Who's Doc," I asked.

Gerry apologized for confusing me.

"Friends and family referred to Doug as Doc. I can't explain that nickname, either. The Richards men had a lot of surprising nicknames. Uncle Joe was known as Dick, which as you know, is usually a nickname for Richard."

I wrote all this down, certain that I wouldn't be able to keep these brothers straight in my mind without a written cast of characters.

Pulling out the Douglas S. Richards obituary, I had her confirm the facts over the phone. Yes, everything in it was true. The Douglas in the obituary was, indeed, her uncle. Her father, Vernie, died just two months after his younger brother did.

Gerry was friendly and talkative. But it wasn't long before she got around to the inevitable question.

"How are you connected to the family?" she asked.

I told her I was an adoptee searching for my biological roots with evidence that Doug Richards was my birth father.

Half expecting her to hang up on me, I was pleasantly surprised when Gerry remained friendly and exhibited genuine interest in my story.

Encouraged to continue, I explained how my mother had been a waitress at Dann's Tavern in 1945 and had gone out with Doug a couple of times. Then I explained the DNA test that suggested my biological surname was Richards.

What Gerry said next took my breath away. "Your situation fascinates me because I've heard this story before."

34

GERRY

I was dumbfounded. What on earth did she mean? Had there been a rumor about me in the Richards family?

It turned out that Gerry was not referring to me at all. Yet the situation she recalled was eerily similar.

In 1952, her father, Vernie, had fathered a son with a waitress from his bar, the Joy Bar. When Gerry heard from me that her uncle might have also fathered a child with a waitress from his bar, it sounded all too familiar.

"My dad supported his son financially," Gerry reflected. "My mother and older sister knew about the boy, but they all kept me in the dark. They thought I was too young and my father did not want to spoil my image of him."

"When did you find out?" I asked, thinking again about all the families I had encountered keeping secrets from their children.

"Just before my dad died in 1986," she responded. "Then my half brother and his family showed up at the funeral!"

Gerry went on to say that twenty-one years had passed and her half brother—who looked a lot like her dad—was fully accepted as a member of the family.

She then shared her feelings.

"Children are not responsible for the actions of their parents. We have to accept the truth as we find it and move on."

I knew Gerry was talking about herself and her brother. Yet her wise words certainly fit my situation as well.

Gerry then asked about my physical appearance. If she could see me in person, she would know if I were a Richards. She was certain of that.

Anxious to pursue my only contact with the family, I asked if she would be willing to meet my wife and me. Her curiosity aroused, Gerry suggested we meet at a restaurant near her home the following Sunday.

Pat and I arrived early and waited for Gerry to arrive. I kept wondering if this possible cousin would look anything like me. When she walked in and looked around, I saw a short, attractive woman with tightly curled, strawberry blonde hair.

No obvious resemblance there, I thought.

I greeted her at the door and showed her to the table where Pat was waiting. After a little bit of small talk, she apologized for meeting in a restaurant.

She explained that her husband had needed a long time to accept her new brother. Predictably, he was less than enthused about her getting involved with my search.

To summarize her husband's position, she passed on two of his favorite expressions: "Let sleeping dogs lie" and "Don't dig up old bones."

"Don't worry," she went on. "He will get used to you just like he did my brother."

"Does that mean you think I'm a Richards?" I asked.

"There's no doubt in my mind," she said.

That was music to my ears. I already had the circumstantial evidence that Doug had dated Jackie and the DNA evidence that my biological surname was Richards. Now I had Gerry's assurance that I looked like a Richards.

Unfortunately, only the first of these three clues pointed directly at Doug Richards...and Gerry was about to muddy the waters.

"I have to wonder," she pondered aloud. "Perhaps my dad was your father."

"What makes you say that?" I asked, surprised that she would raise that possibility.

"You're quite tall and Doug, who we called Doc, was the shortest of the five brothers. My dad was the tallest and I think you look more like him."

She could be right, I realized. Vernie, aka Jack, must have been in his brother's bar from time to time. It was certainly possible—even likely—that Jackie knew him.

Since both men were dead, father-son paternity tests were not an option. Sadly, I realized that a Y-DNA test of their sons could not settle the issue, either. Vernie and Doug had inherited the same Y-chromosome from their father. Then they passed it on to all their male children, including me. We would all match on a Y-DNA test.

I asked Gerry if I could see photos of the men. She had some at home and invited us to follow her there.

When we arrived, Gerry introduced Pat and me to her husband. He was cordial, but he did not join us when we sat down at the kitchen table to look at pictures.

Gerry had lots of photos of her father, of course, and tall, dark-haired Vernie did remind me a lot of myself. She also had one photo of the five brothers standing together as young men.

Brothers Vernie, Clyde, Doug, Joe, and Wayne

"They're in order of age," she explained: "Vernie, Clyde, Doug, Joe, and Wayne. All are gone now. And except for Wayne's widow, all their wives are gone."

Doug was indeed the shortest. And even though the photo was in black and white, I could see that his hair was a bit lighter than that of his brothers. In my opinion, the three who looked the most like me were Vernie, Joe, and Wayne.

"Were any of the other brothers living in Michigan in 1945?" I asked.

"Clyde was here and also married. But he was a schoolteacher and not the kind of man to frequent bars. Joe and Wayne were single then, but I don't know if they were here or in Texas. I'll have to look into that."

Gerry promised to look for other photos and send me copies by mail. Then she brought out something else for me to see: the Richards family Bible.

Obviously quite old and beginning to deteriorate, the Bible had belonged to Gerry's great-grandfather. Born in Alabama in 1835, he had moved to Texas in 1859. Birth and death dates for numerous family members had been recorded by hand in the front and back pages.

I copied down all of the names and dates. Even though my father's identity was still in doubt, I now knew the grandfather and great-grandfather in the paternal line. If I could research that line back another generation or two, perhaps I could connect this Richards line to Wiley's line. Then we would know the common ancestor responsible for our DNA match.

Gerry and I exchanged e-mail addresses and agreed to work together to solve this mystery. I now had an ally within the Richards family...and she seemed as determined as I was to discover the truth.

.

35

FATHERS AND SONS

Gerry and I decided to be discreet about my situation until we could determine all the possible birth father candidates and come up with a plan of action.

Using online genealogy tools, I traced this Richards family from Texas back to Franklin County, North Carolina—the same county where Wiley Richards's ancestor lived about the same time. This supported my assumption that Wiley was connected to me through Gerry's family.

Knowing that the three older Richards brothers lived in or near Livonia at the time Jackie became pregnant, we still needed to learn the whereabouts of the two younger ones.

Joe had served in the Marines, but Gerry unearthed a photo placing him at a family event in the summer of 1945. He could have gone to the bar owned by his Uncle Doug, aka Doc, and met Jackie. What's more, a photo of Joe in his Marine uniform bore a striking resemblance to me in my high school band uniform.

Also, Joe had used the nickname, Dick. If Jackie had known him by that name, she could have suggested the name, Richard, to my adoptive parents. A stretch perhaps, but it was an intriguing thought.

Wayne, the youngest of the brothers, graduated from his Texas high school in June 1945. Gerry found out from his widow that Wayne spent that summer working for Vernie and Doug in Michigan before returning to Texas to join the Army in September.

One of Wayne's jobs was to visit both bars shortly before closing to pick up the day's receipts. Jackie worked Saturday nights and must have met him. She had an ongoing need for a ride home...and Wayne had access to a car.

In just a couple weeks, my suspect list had mushroomed from one guy—Doug—to all five Richards brothers. Granted, Doug was Jackie's employer and any connection between Jackie and the other four was more speculative. But in theory, any one of them could have gotten Jackie pregnant and given me the Y-chromosome that matched Wiley Richards's.

Gerry sent me a copy of the five-brother photo, which I scanned and e-mailed to my kids and several others who were aware of my search. I did not identify anyone or provide any clues. I simply asked, on appearance alone, if any of these men looked like they could be my biological father.

Some people picked one; others thought two of them looked like me. When I added up the votes, Joe and Wayne received seven each. Vernie got three. Doug got one. No one thought it was Clyde.

All reviewers expressed confidence in their choices. Even my cousin who cast the lone vote for Doug felt strongly about her minority opinion. "Without a doubt, you look like the brother in the center!!!!" she wrote. "It's amazing, can you see it? He doesn't appear to be as tall as you, but you could have gotten your height from your uncles."

No, I did not see the resemblance she was seeing. Yet I was glad somebody had voted for Doug. After all, he was the only one of the brothers known to have gone out with my birth mother. In my mind, that single piece of evidence made him a more likely candidate than his siblings, who had merely been in the area.

While the results of my poll were interesting, I knew that opinions on physical appearance could not provide a definitive answer.

DNA had helped me twice before. A paternity test had eliminated Conrad and a Y-DNA test had pointed me to the Richards family. Could another DNA test tell which of these five brothers had fathered me?

Although they were all deceased, each man had at least one living son. One would be my half brother and the others would be cousins. It seemed logical that the half brother, with whom I shared a father, should have more DNA in common with me than cousins who only shared a pair of grandparents.

Searching online, I found a few labs offering a DNA sibling test. The companies I had used for my two prior tests were not among them. I reviewed the two most promising web sites and called each company to discuss my situation.

Each company offered home test kits for situations that did not have legal ramifications. And each one admitted that results of a sibling test were not always conclusive. If I tested sons of all five men, however, the chances were good that one of them would stand out as my half brother.

Could I convince five men to take a DNA test for a complete stranger? Since the goal was to discover the father of an illegitimate child, each man would be playing Russian roulette with his father's reputation.

I had written many persuasive letters in my career and in my search. But this time, anything less than a 100 percent response rate would be a failure.

With great care, I prepared a two-page letter. I summarized the historical events and explained how the Y-DNA test, combined with my genealogy research, suggested that my father had been one of these five brothers. I enclosed photos of myself at various ages along with a photo of Jackie. I wanted them to see what Gerry saw—that I looked like a member of their family.

Next, I explained how the sibling test worked and the painless, at-home sampling procedure. Then I provided the web address of the company I had chosen to do the test. I explained that I would pay all costs of testing and share the results with them.

In closing, I told each man that I would be trying to reach him by phone in a few days to introduce myself and answer any questions he might have. In case anyone wanted to contact me, I provided my home phone, cell phone, e-mail address, and postal mailing address.

Gerry gave me the names and mailing addresses of all five men. She also called her half brother and the two cousins she spoke with most often to tell them about me in advance, expressing her opinion that I was definitely a Richards.

On April 10, 2007, I sent out all five letters and photo sets in Priority Mail envelopes so they would stand out from the usual junk mail. On the following weekend, I began making my phone calls.

I decided to start with Gerry's brother, Vern. The situation surrounding his birth was so similar to mine that I felt certain he would be sympathetic.

A restaurant manager, Vern was living in Alabama. He had received my mailing and was expecting my call.

Vern agreed with Gerry that I had to be a Richards. He could see himself and Wayne's son, Dale, in my college graduation photo. He went on to tell me his story.

He saw Vernie a lot as he was growing up, but thought the man was merely a friend of the family. He was a teenager when an older brother told him that Vernie was his father. Angry at first, he went to military school and then into the Army for six years. Once he got over his anger, he enjoyed a good relationship with Vernie and legally changed his name to Vern Richards.

Vernie had been a successful man, owned a large number of racehorses, and always attracted a lot of attention from the ladies. Vern said it would not surprise him at all if his father turned out to be my father.

Vern had no problem taking the DNA test and said he would be glad to help me.

One down, four to go.

The next one I spoke with was Clyde's son, Dave. A former science teacher who had retired to northern Michigan, Dave was fascinated by the Y-DNA test I had done and the DNA sibling test I proposed to do.

Having already spoken with Gerry, he was on board with the idea of me being a member of the family and was quite willing to be included in the sibling test. He thought I looked a lot like his Uncle Vernie.

We both agreed that Dave's father was the least likely of the brothers to have been involved with Jackie. Gerry had already described Clyde as a schoolteacher who did not spend time in bars. Dave concurred. Unlike Vernie and Doug, Clyde had never been one to fool around. He didn't even have a cool nickname like Jack or Doc.

Thinking about the nicknames used by three of the brothers, I asked Dave what he knew about that. The only one he could explain was Doc. "All those kids were born at home," he said. "The only exception was Doug, who was a difficult delivery and had to be born in a hospital. As I heard it, that's how he got the nickname Doc."

Dave informed me that the Richards family would be having a reunion at his place on July 21. He suggested that my wife and I plan to attend. That way I could meet a number of family members in person.

Gladly, I accepted his kind invitation. That gave me a hard deadline. I had just over three months to complete DNA testing and prove my relationship to this family.

Two down, three to go.

The three remaining guys were all in Texas. I decided to start with Wayne's son, Dale, the last of the three that Gerry had primed to receive my call. Gerry had warned me not to mistake Dale's strong Texas accent for a lack of intelligence. A successful rancher, he was, in her words, "one smart cookie."

I had never known a rancher and I looked forward to our conversation. When I did reach him, I learned that Dale had a keen interest in family history. He was eager to hear about his great-grandfather's parents, who I had identified and traced back to North Carolina.

Dale's father, Wayne, had returned from his stint in the Army to get married, run the family ranch, and look after his aging parents. Dale grew up on the ranch and stayed there. Buying ten cows and a bull when he was eleven, he had owned cattle continuously since then.

Exactly like me, Dale enjoyed math and science in high school and went to college on a scholarship to study physics.

That was my major, I reflected with amazement.

But Dale was an outdoor guy, not a classroom guy. So he quit college and became a professional firefighter for thirty-five years, while continuing as a rancher.

Like his father was decades ago, Dale was active in his community and had been elected to serve on the local school board.

I learned that Dale's father, Wayne, had caught rheumatic fever twice as a child, which led to serious cardiac problems. He died at age thirty-eight after complications from heart surgery.

Based on the photos I had sent him, Dale thought I fit in well with the family. In his opinion, I most resembled Vernie, but he was open to the possibility that his father could have been mine.

"If I was in your situation," Dale said, "I would want to know."

He then agreed to take the DNA test and promised to see me at the Richards reunion.

Three down, two to go.

Everyone I had spoken with so far was friendly and open to the possibilities suggested by my story. There was no doubt, however, that Gerry had favorably influenced the first three men before I ever got them on the phone.

Would I get the same treatment from the last two guys, who merely opened their mail one day to find my letter and photos?

36

BLUES

The next man I reached by phone was Doug Richards Jr. He had received the package and examined the photos.

"Your story is real interesting," he said right off. "I commend you for looking into it."

He was quick to admit that his father had a reputation for sleeping around in his younger days, though he settled down later in life.

"He must have changed," I observed. "I understand he was married for fifty years."

"My mother used to say that the first twenty-five years with my dad were the toughest, but the last twenty-five were a breeze."

I suggested that my letter must have come as a shock. He disagreed.

"My sister, Elaine, and I had actually talked about this possibility. With our dad it wasn't a question of *would* another child contact us someday...it was only a question of *when*. In that sense, your letter was expected."

By the tone of his voice, I could tell he was not upset. If anything, he seemed to find the situation mildly amusing.

Doug went on to say that his wife thought he and I looked some-what alike, but he did not see it.

Although his dad was only five foot ten, there was a lot of height in the Richards family. Uncle Vernie was over six feet tall. Doug Jr. said he was six foot one.

Having recently spoken with Dale, I noted that Doug did not sound like a Texan. It turns out that Doug's family returned to Michigan for awhile in the fifties. He had also served in the Army. So his speech reflected a blend of Midwestern and other influences.

We continued to talk about the Richards family history. He told me how Uncle Vernie had been loading railroad ties in Houston and ended up in Florida. He met a guy in a bar that suggested he come along on a ship going to Detroit. It was a Ford-owned ship and that was how Vernie ended up working for Ford in Detroit.

When Vernie's brothers, Clyde and Doug, heard about the opportu-nities in Detroit and the Henry Ford Trade school, they also moved to Michigan.

"Before he got into the bar business, my dad was a tool and die maker for Ford," Doug noted.

That was an interesting coincidence, I thought. My adoptive father had been a tool and die maker for Oldsmobile.

I told Doug Jr. that I had been doing some genealogy work to extend the Richards family tree farther back in time. Doug was quick to comment.

"Uncle Vernie once paid a genealogist three hundred dollars to uncover the family's history." For a second, I thought he was serious. But he continued.

"Then he paid him three thousand dollars to cover it up again!"

I laughed, but Doug did not know me well enough to be sure I got it.

"That's a joke," he said.

We finished our conversation with Doug agreeing to take the DNA test and telling me that he planned to be in Michigan for the Richards reunion. That meant we could meet face to face in July.

Four down, one to go.

I tried to call Joe Jr., but kept getting his answering machine. Eventually, I left my name and phone number but nothing more. This was not something I wanted to discuss by machine.

When a week went by without any word from Joe, I began to worry that my luck had run out. Gerry had said Joe was an orthodontist. Maybe he was just busy. Then my phone rang and it was Joe.

He had just caught up on his mail, including my letter. In his opinion, my pictures did suggest I was a Richards, though he was not sure which of the brothers I resembled most.

My conversations with Dale and Doug Jr. had made me more conscious than usual of regional accents. Joe did have a slight Texas accent, just not as pronounced as Dale's. I thought of it as Texas-lite.

He started to tell me that his father, Joe Sr., spent World War II in the Pacific and could not have been in Michigan. But then I heard Joe's wife interrupting him.

She had just pulled Joe Sr.'s military records from their files and was checking his service dates. He joined in November 1943 and was discharged in March 1946. Yet there was something in the file they had never noticed before.

The Marines had granted Joe a thirty-day emergency leave in August 1945. Then they extended it twice to ninety days.

Joe Jr. was stunned. He had not known about that and he had no idea where Joe Sr. spent that leave time. Since much of the family was in Michigan by 1945, it could have been there.

It must have been Michigan, I thought, remembering Gerry's comment that Joe Sr. was included in a family photo taken that summer.

"My parents did not get married until 1947, so all of this was well before my time," he said.

As for the DNA test, Joe said he would be happy to help in any way he could. Then he became the first man to express an opinion on the outcome.

"For your sake, I hope my dad was not your father," he said.

"Why is that?" I asked.

"Because he was mentally ill," Joe explained. "He spent a lot of time in VA hospitals. People say he was normal before the war, but the father I knew had serious problems with temperament and ambition."

Joe went on to say that Uncle Vernie had even provided his father with a bar to run, but he couldn't handle the responsibility.

"Was that the Oasis, which became the Good Time Bar?" I asked.

"I think it was," Joe replied.

"We would have starved if the rest of the family had not helped us out so much. And my brother and I would not have gone to college and dental school without financial help from Uncle Vernie and Uncle Doc."

Joe went on to say that his father had been in some of the bloodiest battles in the Pacific islands. Doctors today would probably classify his mental health issues as post-traumatic stress disorder. But back then, nobody knew what to call it, let alone how to treat it.

Most likely, the emergency leave in 1945 had something to do with this condition.

Joe also hoped that Wayne did not prove to be my father, because Wayne's widow was still alive. They did not get married until Wayne got out of the Army, but they had been high school sweethearts and Joe thought they might have been engaged at the time my birth mother got pregnant.

I understood what he was saying. But I knew there was nothing I could do about the outcome of my DNA test. The die had been cast more than sixty years ago. All I could do now was learn the truth and try to smooth over any hurt feelings that might occur.

I asked Joe if he would be at the Richards reunion. He said he never attended because it was always in summer.

"That's peak season for kids' braces. I can't take time off in the summer."

We then wrapped up the conversation, said good-bye, and ended the call.

Five down, none to go!

Now that all five men had agreed to do the DNA sibling test, I phoned Gerry to share the good news. Not only had they agreed to be tested...I enjoyed the time I'd spent speaking with each of them.

I knew I would be pleased and proud to have any of them as a brother or cousin.

Gerry added that I could not go wrong with any of the men's fathers being my father. Wayne's heart problems and Joe's mental health issues were not genetic. They simply resulted from unfortunate events in their lives.

I responded that Doug, aka Doc, my mother's employer at Dann's Tavern, was still the most likely candidate, since I knew she had gone out with him.

Gerry told me that her Uncle Doc had been an excellent business-man. She remembered that he once had a big nightclub in Texas where well-known entertainers like Redd Foxx performed.

"Uncle Doc was not just successful. He was incredibly family ori-ented," she said. "When he was alive, he practically demanded that everyone attend family reunions."

"Since everyone knew how generous he could be with his money," Gerry laughed, "they usually showed up."

Gerry then told me she had mailed some more pictures that showed her father and uncles later in life. The photos arrived the next day.

She had previously described the men in her father's family as "bar-rel-chested." As I looked at the photos of these men, probably in their sixties, I noticed some barrels, but they were no longer around their chests.

Considering the era in which these men lived, I guessed that most of them smoked cigarettes and lived on high-fat diets. I had never been a smoker. Furthermore, I had a wife who studied good nutrition and practiced it in the food she prepared.

Looking at these pictures, I appreciated Pat's efforts even more. Thanks mostly to her, I had defied genetics and delayed the expansion of my waistline.

Gerry had thoughtfully identified the men in each photo. Seeing my first color photo of the man they called Doc, I remarked how much he reminded me of my adopted father in his later years.

Now that was a coincidence! He had the same build, wore his gray-ing hair in the same crew cut, and had the same steel blue eyes.

Immediately, I sensed my body tensing up. Something was wrong. Then, I remembered what it was.

37

DECISIONS

Way back in 1964, on the day I learned about my adoption, I had remembered a DNA lesson from high school biology. Brown eyes were dominant. Blue eyes were recessive. And two blue-eyed parents should not produce a brown-eyed child. For me, that memory had confirmed the truth of my adoption.

Jackie had not lived long enough to reach the era when color photography became commonplace. But her sister and friends had all mentioned my birth mother's beautiful blue eyes. Since I have light brown eyes, my birth father's eyes could not also have been blue.

The conclusion was obvious. Doug Richards, Jackie's employer at Dann's Tavern and my number one suspect, could not be my father.

Having heard so many good things about "Uncle Doc," my opinion of the man had been rising. Eliminating him now reminded me of the feeling I had when the paternity test proved Conrad was not my father.

I checked all the other men in the photos and then called Gerry. She confirmed that Doug had been the only brother with blue eyes. The other four had brown eyes.

Faced with this confidence-shaking piece of information, my thoughts turned negative. What if I had the wrong Richards family? Worse yet, what if my Y-DNA match was just a meaningless fluke? Maybe I was not even a Richards. Could I start all over again? More to the point, would I even want to start all over again?

I had only been talking to Gerry and her family for a few weeks. Yet in my heart and mind, I had already adopted them as my family. Plus, I was about to order several expensive DNA tests.

The lab I had decided to use was fully accredited and charged less for a sibling test than the other finalist did.

I called and the woman I spoke with gave me a pricing tip that helped. The cost of adding extra people was the same whether I ordered them all at once or added some later.

That was a relief. I could start small.

As I asked her about the blue-eye issue, it became obvious that she was in sales and had limited understanding of DNA. It took a little convincing, but she let me speak to a guy in the lab.

Explaining my overall situation and test objective, I reviewed my understanding of eye colors and re-stated my question.

"Is it impossible for a blue-eyed man to have been my father?"

The technician responded that "impossible" was too strong a word. A better word was "unlikely." The impact of genetics on physical appearance was incredibly complex. The simplistic two-gene model I learned in high school could not reliably predict traits like eye color and mutations were always possible.

I couldn't help but notice that his response was essentially what Mrs. Stewart told me after biology class in 1962!

"I can't tell you what to do," he continued. "But if it were me, I would spend my money testing sons of the brown-eyed guys first."

Thanking him for his time, I transferred back to the sales person and placed my order. Test kits would be shipped to me and the first three potential brothers with whom I had spoken: Vern, Dave, and Dale, who represented their fathers Vernie, Clyde, and Wayne.

I almost omitted Dave, since his father's appearance and upright behavior suggested that Clyde was not my father. But my science training kicked in at the last minute. As a presumed cousin, Dave would be a good control subject for comparing the results I got from the others.

Worst case, if none of these three guys was related to me, I would save some money by not testing Joe Jr. and Doug Jr.

We all had to receive and submit our test kits. Then it would be a few more weeks before the results would be ready. In the meantime, the Michigan branch of the family began to check me out.

Dave and his wife were going to be passing through Grand Rapids and they wanted to meet us. We had them stop by our home for lunch. Within minutes, it felt like the four of us had known each other for years. On their way out, they invited us to spend a weekend with them at their northern Michigan home in June.

Not long after that, Gerry made the trip to our side of the state and spent a day with us. Her husband did not accompany her on this first trip, but he joined her on a later visit and we could tell by then that he was getting used to us.

At some point, Dave, and then Gerry, each found an old genealogy report that someone had prepared covering all the lines of the Richards family. It had been around a long time and neither could remember who put it together. Each made copies and sent it to me.

When I saw the report, I remembered the joke Doug Jr. had made. Maybe there was a grain of truth to that story. Maybe Vernie did hire a genealogist.

Whoever did the research used standard genealogy forms and filled in the information by hand. It covered every branch of the family, including the wives of my possible grandfather and great-grandfather.

Whether this family proved to be mine or not, I wanted to go to the July reunion bearing some kind of gift in return for their kindness. I decided to research the family, update what I could, and generate computerized genealogy reports for everyone.

I purchased Family Tree Maker, a genealogy program, and entered all the data from the old sheets. I then added the new information on the great-great-grandparents that I had discovered myself. Finally, I got a one-year subscription to Ancestry.com, a service that collects genealogy records and provides them online. That let me fill in some more blank spots.

After working on the family tree of this family, I wanted to do the same for my birth mother's family and my wife's family. At sixty years of age, I had discovered a passion for genealogy.

———◆———

May arrived and the sibling test results were still not ready. Pat and I took a two-week vacation to Nevada and Arizona. The last thing on our agenda was a four-night stay at the south rim of the Grand Canyon. Throughout the trip, I had been checking my Blackberry for an e-mail from the DNA lab. But once we got inside the national park, I had zero service. No phone. No e-mail.

Each evening, after hiking and sightseeing all day, I dragged my tired body to the lobby of the lodge. I pushed dollar bills into the computer's pay slot and logged in to my e-mail account. Still, there was no message from the lab.

On the last day of our vacation, we left the park, drove south to the interstate, and headed west toward the airport in Las Vegas. As we got within range of the cell phone towers, my phone began to download five days of accumulated e-mails.

At a refueling stop before the Arizona-Nevada border, I saw three automated messages from the lab, one for each comparison. Each message had a test report attached.

Finally, I thought. The big moment I've been waiting for.

At that point, I didn't care which guy turned out to be my half brother. The only bad result—and one that I still feared—would be a weak match with everyone. That would tell me I was testing the wrong family.

Barely able to breathe, I opened the first document and began to read it on the tiny screen of my Blackberry.

38

RESULTS

I started with the report on Vern. If blue eyes eliminated Doug Sr., I felt my next best suspect was Vern's father, Vernie. He was the tallest of the brothers and a few people in the family thought I resembled him the most.

There was a table of numbers too big to view on my phone. But I could read the all-important Half Sibling Index. I knew that a score of 1.0 indicated a 50 percent chance that he and I were half siblings. Any number greater than one would mean a higher probability and a number less than one would reflect a lower probability.

I found my Half Sibling Index with Vern was 0.67.

Ouch. That was not high enough to make us half siblings. I wondered if it was enough to confirm a cousin relationship. I didn't know.

Next, I checked Dave's report. Incredibly, the index was 2.32.

I was thrilled to see a number that high. This was black-and-white proof that I had found the right family!

On the other hand, no one would believe that Dave's father, the straight-arrow Clyde, was my father. There had to be a still higher score.

Anxiously, I opened the last report. The index with Dale was 4.69! This was a strong indication that his father, Wayne, could have been my father.

With a huge sigh of relief, I shared the results with Pat and we toasted this good news at the gas station with a fresh purchase of bottled water. I wanted to call the family right away. But with a plane to catch in Las Vegas, we had to get back on the road.

The day after we arrived home, I printed the three complete reports and looked at the details behind the Half Sibling Index numbers. As of now, Dale's DNA was most like mine. But I still had two guys untested.

There was no doubt that I had to test Joe Jr. But these tests were expensive and I wondered if it was necessary to test Doug Jr. due to his father's blue eyes.

After giving it some thought, I decided to save the money. I called the lab and only ordered one more kit—for Joe.

I e-mailed Gerry and called all the guys to share the results of the first tests. While I had Doug Jr. on the phone, I explained why I decided to omit him. To my surprise, he seemed hurt and disappointed.

"What if I pay for the test myself?" he asked.

Amazed that he cared so much, I could not refuse his offer. I called the lab back and ordered another kit for Doug. Now we would all know that I had checked every possibility.

———◆———

About a week later, the postman delivered a large mailing tube to our door. Addressed to me, it bore Gerry's return address. I opened the tube and unrolled a huge piece of poster board. In the center, she had written the following message in large letters:

"Welcome to the Richards Family!"

Around the edges were eleven snapshots of various family members, each one captioned with names. She had covered the rest of the poster with stars, glitter, and other signs of celebration.

I was touched. Even shocked.

Never in my wildest dreams had I imagined a reception like the one I was getting from this family. I called Gerry and expressed my most sincere thanks.

In early June, Pat and I followed up on the earlier invitation and went up north for a weekend with Dave Richards and his wife. They loved nature and enjoyed being in the presence of deer, bears, and the bald eagles that soared over the small lake in front of their home. Just outside their windows, Dave had the largest collection of bird feeders Pat and I had ever seen. It was a wonderful weekend.

Shortly after our return, I learned from Gerry that Dale had told his mother, Mattie, about the preliminary test results. Mattie responded that the family had accepted Vern before and they would welcome me, as well.

This was extremely gracious of her, I thought.

If Dale was indeed my half sibling, it had to mean that Mattie's boyfriend and future husband, Wayne, had been involved with another woman during his summer in Michigan.

I decided to write to Mattie and introduce myself. I sent her the photos that I had mailed to the five test subjects—this time omitting the one of my birth mother. My letter explained how I got involved in my search and how my birth mother's job at Doug's bar gave her the opportunity to meet Wayne.

About a week later, Mattie called our home and I had a nice conversation with her. I learned that she and Wayne had dated on and off since their early teens. They broke up many times over an eight-year period and always got back together. She said she could not object to anything that happened before they were married.

Mattie noted that my resemblance to her son was not obvious, because Dale was a lot heavier than I was. She said he got his weight from her side of the family. I told her I looked forward to meeting them both at the reunion.

Less than a week after Mattie's call, I received another surprise package in the mail. This time it was a photo album with captioned pictures of Wayne, Mattie, Dale, and his two sisters at various times in their lives.

Once again, the good-heartedness of my new family left me almost speechless.

I called Mattie to thank her. She gave much of the credit to her daughter, who had created the captions on her computer.

Sadly, Mattie reported that she was having health problems and would not make it to the reunion.

While all this was going on, my efforts to expand the family tree were progressing. I met a distant cousin in an online genealogy forum. His ancestor and my great-great-grandfather were brothers. I learned that a third brother had served in the Texas War of Independence and died at Goliad three weeks after the fall of the Alamo.

The father of these three brothers was born in Virginia in 1742 and was a captain in the Revolutionary War. Unfortunately, the paper trail ended with him. During the Civil War, the Union Army burned the Virginia courthouse containing his family's birth, marriage, and death records.

As a frustrated genealogist, this Northerner finally understood what Southerners meant by the phrase "damn Yankees."

Admitting I had reached a brick wall on the family tree, I took what I had and prepared my genealogy report for the Richards family reunion.

The question of my birth father's ethnicity was pretty much settled. I had learned that Richards was originally a Welsh name, but it had spread throughout the British Isles. So it was highly likely that the Richards family came from England as did many of the Virginia colonists. Some of the other lines in my birth father's family were clearly traceable to Ireland and there was even one from Sweden.

There was not a trace of Polish.

———◆———

Four days before the reunion, I received an e-mail with Joe's DNA results attached. My Half-Sibling Index with him was 4.12. This was nearly as high as Dale's 4.69. Suddenly, the results were not as clear-cut as they had looked earlier.

I called the lab and asked for the technician I had spoken with previously. When I told him the index numbers, he said all were high enough to indicate a family relationship. But Dale's lead over the others was not large enough to isolate him as my half sibling.

"How much difference does it take to be sure?" I asked.

"Comparing a half sibling to cousins, I like to see one index number at least three times greater than all the others."

Hanging up the phone, I realized I had a predicament. Dale, Joe, or even Dave could be my half sibling. Yet the whole family had concluded that Dale was my brother, since he had the highest score.

I didn't know what to do next. There was a slim chance that Doug's Half Sibling Index would come in much higher than the rest. But Doug currently had bigger concerns than my DNA test. Due to extensive flooding in his part of Texas, water was inching closer to his home. He had not yet sent in his sample and would not be coming to the reunion.

I barely had time to reflect on all this when Gerry called.

Dale had arrived in Michigan. Even though the reunion was that weekend, he wanted to visit our home Thursday so he could meet me ahead of time.

I looked forward with excitement to meeting Dale. Yet the situation was still unclear. We could be siblings or cousins. Apparently, this was going to be a lot more complex than finding Mike, my brother on my mother's side, twenty-five years earlier.

39

REUNION

On Thursday, July 19, 2007, Gerry and Dale arrived at our house as planned. Our daughter, Catherine, was in the area and she joined us for this special occasion.

Gerry and I handled the introductions and I shook hands with the man who might be my brother. Dale was several inches shorter than I was but at least forty pounds heavier. He wore jeans, cowboy boots, and a ten-gallon hat. He also had a warm smile and a twinkle in his eyes.

It was a beautiful summer day but too windy to sit on the deck for long. We settled down inside and began the process of getting to know each other. Dale spoke with the kind of courtesy we rarely experience from anyone but members of the military. We heard a lot of "yes, sir" and "no, ma'am" delivered in his rich Texas accent.

Dale brought a framed, high school graduation photo of his father, Wayne. Formally attired in a suit and wearing glasses, Wayne looked scholarly. This was an entirely different look than I had seen in snapshots.

I brought out a studio photo of me, taken as a young boy, and laid it next to Wayne's picture. The resemblance was extraordinary. We compared the hair, eyes, ears, mouth, and chin. Everything seemed to match.

"You look more like my daddy than I do," Dale remarked.

In this comparison, anyway, he was correct. This obvious match in appearance increased everyone's confidence that Wayne had been my father.

The photo was Dale's only copy. Carefully, I removed the picture from its frame. I then scanned it into my computer and returned it to the frame.

Catherine used my camera to take some photos of Dale, Gerry, Pat, and me plus some more of just Dale and me together. We even got Dale to remove his big hat for one. Gerry joked that this would be one of the few photos in existence of Dale without a hat.

Eventually, we all sat down for the excellent dinner that Pat prepared and had a chance to learn more about Dale, his family history, and life on the ranch. I was fascinated with Dale's stories and looked forward to confirming that he was, indeed, my brother.

After they left, Pat and I began preparing for the Richards reunion.

During our June stay with Dave, he had pointed out a small campground where Gerry and her husband planned to park their trailer during the reunion. Dale carried a tent in the back of his truck and would be staying there, too. Pat and I still had a pop-up camper that we had not used much since moving to the lake. Deciding to camp with the others, we got it out of storage.

On Friday afternoon, we towed our camper north and that evening we set up camp next to Gerry and Dale. Dave had reserved a hunting lodge for the reunion on Saturday and Sunday. With children and grandchildren, there were close to thirty people in attendance.

Our son, Mark, drove up for the day on Saturday. Before he left, he was able to take part in a family tradition at Dave's place: slowly driving the dirt roads at dusk to spot white-tailed deer. Except for the deer spotting, it was a typical family reunion with lots of food, conversation, and various group photos.

Several people played a dominoes game called "42," which is apparently as big in Texas as the card game Euchre (pronounced "you-ker") is in Michigan. I watched for awhile, but they played so fast I could not make sense of it. Then on Saturday night, we had a huge bonfire behind the lodge.

All weekend, people were interested in meeting me and hearing my story. Naturally, I was excited to meet them, share my experience, and learn more about my newfound family.

Dave, the weekend's host, humorously lamented to one and all that he had lost what he christened the "Win-a-Brother Contest."

Besides Dale, the apparent "winner," only three other people made it all the way from Texas. As expected, Joe, Doug, and Mattie were not there. But Gerry's brother, Vern, and his wife drove up from Alabama.

I thanked Vern for being the pioneer. There was no doubt in my mind that his surprise appearance as Vernie's son twenty-one years earlier had pre-conditioned people to believe my story and accept me as a member of the family.

When I gave out my genealogy report, I learned that Vern's wife was responsible for the genealogy research I had used to get started. The story about Vernie paying someone to explore the family tree really was just a joke. Vern's wife had done it for free.

Vern pulled his old high school ID card out of his wallet and showed it to me. Although he was now much heavier than I was, we had once looked remarkably alike. To me, that added even more evidence that I had found the biological family of my birth father.

On the other hand, it reminded me that I still lacked conclusive proof that Dale's father, Wayne, had been my father.

Late Saturday night at the campground, Dale and I stood outside talking in the moonlight. Just before we turned in for the night, he had one more thing he wanted to say.

"I would be proud to have you as my brother," Dale said. "But I'm the kind of guy that needs everything in black and white. I want a yes or no answer on this. After my momma is gone, I'm prepared to have my daddy's body dug up so we can get some of his DNA."

For a few seconds, I was speechless. Yes, I also wanted to know for sure. But I could live with a measure of doubt rather than have someone's body exhumed.

Already, I knew Dale well enough to understand why he would not hesitate to share this idea. He was a straight shooter in every way, speaking his mind without regard to the popularity of his opinion. That was one reason people admired him so much.

Then I remembered one of the expressions that Gerry had attributed to her husband: "Don't dig up old bones." He meant it in a figurative sense, of course. What would he and the rest of the family think if we did it literally?

I told Dale that I hoped such a drastic step would not be necessary. There had to be another answer.

40

BLOOD

A few weeks after the Richards reunion, Pat and I met again with some of my high school classmates. Joe Stewart was there and I presented him with a bottle of his favorite scotch. I then explained to the group how his tip about the Y-DNA test had led me to my birth father's family.

One of the women asked me if I was going to change my name. "You could be Richard Richards," she said with a smile. I told her I would pass on that opportunity.

By this time, the lab had received Doug's test kit and I was anxious to know his results. I kept calling the lab every Friday and the people I spoke with kept telling me that the results would go out in the next few days. It never happened. Weeks passed.

In late August, at long last, someone told me the results would go out within an hour. I checked e-mail all evening and got nothing, so I gave up around 10:30 and went to bed. At 12:40 a.m., I still couldn't sleep so I got up and checked my computer again. The e-mail had come in at 10:47—just after I stopped checking.

Doug's score was 3.80, putting him in third place.

A good score, I thought. But I still didn't have one score three times greater than the others.

With Doug having such a strong score, I now had four of the five men looking like possible brothers—an impossible and frustrating result.

How could this be?

The next day I called the lab again and asked to speak with my technical contact. There was a table of numbers in each report that I could not follow and I wanted to understand the workings of the test.

He explained that everyone has two numbers for each tested marker, e.g. ten and twelve. Each parent passes on one of his or her two numbers to each child. Since the process is random, even full siblings may not end up with the same pair of numbers on every marker.

The index numbers reflect how well we match on that marker and how rare our values are in our racial group. Matching on a rare value is less likely to be accidental, so that earns a higher index number. Finally, all the index numbers are multiplied together to arrive at a Half Sibling Index.

My Half Sibling Index numbers were all high enough to indicate a family relationship:

Dale	4.69
Joe	4.12
Doug	3.80
Dave	2.32
Vern	0.67

Unfortunately, no one stood out with a score that was at least three times bigger than the others.

After the call, I kept reviewing the data. For the first time, I noticed that each report had eleven rows of data representing eleven markers. That number did not seem right.

Re-checking the sibling test description on the lab's web site, I discovered what was bothering me. The sibling test was supposed to use sixteen markers, not eleven.

I redialed the number of the lab. I'm sure they were tired of hearing from me, but I had to get to the bottom of this.

As usual, the first person I reached was someone in sales. She explained that one marker merely indicated gender, leaving fifteen markers for a complete comparison.

Checking my file, she confirmed that samples from four of the guys were complete. Joe's sample, however, was missing two markers. More important, four markers were missing from my sample.

Since they only had eleven markers from me, all reports comparing me to others could only be based on eleven markers.

"This can occur from bacteria on food particles in the mouth," she said. "Plus, some people don't have enough saliva to provide a good sample."

"Then we need to submit new samples," I said.

"That would not make any difference in your results," she stated flatly.

Fortunately, I had learned enough to know she was wrong. Rather than argue with her, I asked to speak to my contact in the lab.

When I told him that my reports only used eleven markers, he gave me the correct answer.

"You and Joe need to be retested. Those extra four markers could make a big difference in your results."

My anger rising, I told him two things that annoyed me about their service. "First, nobody bothered to inform me that markers were missing. I had to catch that myself and I nearly missed it." Without waiting for a response, I went on. "Then your salesperson told me—incorrectly—that the extra markers would not make a difference."

He apologized. Then he explained that most of their business was in paternity testing, where they sometimes got a definitive answer in the first eight to ten markers. In those cases, the extra markers really did not matter.

"In a sibling test, however, you're dealing in probabilities. Every marker has the potential to significantly change the overall result."

He went on to explain that a standard saliva kit, while easy and painless, might produce incomplete results again. To make sure this re-test would be the final round, he suggested using blood. The cost would be the same, but blood would assuredly capture all the markers.

Anxious to get this settled, I agreed. They would send Joe and me blood-test kits to be sure they could read all our markers. This kit required pricking a finger and letting a few drops of blood fall on a piece of special paper.

I paid for two re-tests plus overnight shipping. My total investment in these sibling tests had now climbed to seven hundred fifty dollars. Yet I no longer cared how much I was spending. I had to get the correct answer.

Hanging up, I called Joe's number and left a message to explain why a blood test kit was coming his way. He called back later to say that was fine with him.

"I'm a dentist," he deadpanned. "I'm not afraid of blood."

When my kit arrived, the instructions suggested using a lancet for pricking the finger. I went to the drug store and discovered I had to buy them by the box.

I only need one, I thought. What am I going to do with all the others?

Well, I was a little off on that. Although I was able to poke holes in my finger, I could not get any of them to bleed. I had to be doing something wrong, I fumed. This should be easy.

Eventually, after many failed attempts and more lancets than I ever dreamed I would need, I forced three drops of blood to fall on the card. I followed the packing instructions and mailed the kit back to the lab on the fifth day of September, 2007.

Instead of comparing me to each man on only eleven markers, the lab would now be able to use all fifteen markers. I realized that the more detailed results could completely revise the order of my scores. Any one of the five men could rise to the top and prove to be my half brother. And any one of their fathers could still be my biological father.

As we discussed this, Pat raised an interesting question. "Which one do you want it to be?" she asked.

Her question made me think. At first, I had wanted my father to be one of the two single guys, because I thought it reflected better on Jackie, my birth mother.

Wayne was one of them and our pictures revealed a strong resemblance. The only thing that bothered me about Wayne being my father was his widow, Mattie. Even though they were not yet married in 1945, the thought of her childhood sweetheart being with Jackie had to be unpleasant.

One of my search goals was not to hurt anyone...and Mattie was the only spouse around to feel the pain inherent in the truth of my birth.

On the other hand, I was already comfortable with the idea of Dale as my brother. So my feelings about Wayne as my father were decidedly mixed.

Joe Sr., the other single guy, had been a Marine. I would be proud to have a Marine veteran as my father. His mental health issues were a product of war and not something genetic. His son, Joe, clearly had his head together because he had become a successful orthodontist. So that outcome would be fine with me.

I realized that I had become comfortable with Vernie/Jack or Doug/Doc being my father. I now knew that both were highly intelligent men who loved their families and generously shared the fruits of their success.

Since the family was already aware of their penchant for infidelity, I didn't think that proof of an affair with Jackie would surprise or upset anyone.

The passage of time helped a lot. Since these men, their wives, and Jackie had been deceased for so long, events from sixty years ago were viewed as history rather than scandal.

The only man I clearly did not want to see as my father was Clyde. There was nothing wrong with him and I knew his son, Dave, would make a great brother. But Clyde was the only outcome that would be totally unexpected. An affair would be completely out of character for him, and I did not want my DNA test to sully his reputation.

Once again, I began to get anxious for the results. On the twenty-sixth day of September, I called the lab. The raw data was ready for analysis.

I suspect the people who answered the phone were aware of my earlier complaints because the woman I spoke with offered to have someone calculate the five Half Sibling Index numbers and call me back in about ten minutes. I thanked her and waited by the phone.

In those moments, I reflected back on this eventful year.

Incredibly, more than five months had passed since I ordered the first sibling tests. More than six months had flown by since I first talked to Gerry. And it was eight months since my Y-DNA test indicated that my biological father's surname was Richards.

The phone rang and the caller ID showed it was the lab. One of the five tested men was my half sibling...and his father had been mine, too. Would the results now be conclusive? I answered the phone.

41

REVISIONS

The caller was not the lab guy I usually spoke with, but he had just calculated my Half Sibling Index numbers based on all fifteen markers.

I knew the earlier scores by heart. How much would they change? "Go ahead," I said. He began to read the results.

"For you and Dave, the Half Sibling Index is .049." Wow, I thought. That dropped from 2.32 in the first test. That's a lot.

"For you and Dale, it's 0.52." What a turnaround from 4.69 in the first test! The early leader and I must have had awfully little in common over the last four markers.

"For you and Joe, it's 1.26." That was 4.12 in the first test. These three scores all went down. But at least I still had one possible brother with a score greater than one.

"For you and Vern, it's 1.49." Vern's score actually went up significantly from 0.67 in the first test.

My mind raced. Now I had two possible brothers, yet neither one stood out. Would my results be just as inconclusive as before? I said a silent prayer that the last one would settle it.

"The final index is for you and Doug. The Half Sibling Index is 6.98." Six point nine eight, I thought. Six point nine eight! That nearly doubled from the 3.80 in the first test!

Tapping the keys on my calculator, I quickly divided Doug's 6.98 by the second closest score of 1.49. Doug's score was 4.7 times bigger.

Almost giddy with excitement, I rushed to confirm the conclusion that was staring me in the face.

I told the man on the phone what the other lab technician had said before: that the half brother's index should be at least three times that of the cousins' to be conclusive.

"I use that same rule of thumb," he replied. "If only one person is tested, I like to see an index number of ten or more. But 6.98 is pretty good when you consider that the only other candidates all scored lower."

"So, Doug is my half brother," I went on, "even though eye color and general physical appearance might suggest otherwise."

The technician chuckled. "The markers we test have nothing to do with physical traits. Anyway, appearance is often a poor indicator of relatedness. Look at it this way," he went on. "DNA trumps physical appearance."

I thanked him for taking the time to call me with the results. Then I reviewed my new Half Sibling Index numbers, based on *all* the markers:

Doug	Son of Doug Sr., aka Doc	6.98
Vern	Son of Vernie, aka Jack	1.49
Joe	Son of Joe Sr., aka Dick	1.26
Dale	Son of Wayne	0.52
Dave	Son of Clyde	0.049

I immediately shared the good news with Pat. "The results are in," I said. "They say that Doug Richards Sr. was my birth father. So his son, Doug Jr., and daughter, Elaine, are my half siblings!"

After several minutes of celebration, Pat had a suggestion. "Maybe you should refer to your birth father as Doc like everyone else does. Then you don't have to keep saying senior or junior to distinguish between him and his son."

"Good idea," I replied. "Doc was my father. Doug is my brother. I like the sound of that."

That day, when the last piece of my puzzle seemed to fall neatly into place, was September 26, 2007, twenty-six years after starting my search.

Looking back, I remembered the many people who helped me. Then I thought of all the crazy, lucky breaks that somehow got me to the next step.

To say the least, I was incredibly thankful.

My path had been far from smooth. Family secrecy, the closed adoption file, lies, false rumors, and my own periods of inactivity caused enormous delays. Then I had to wait for the development of a whole new science called genetic genealogy.

The outcome wasn't perfect, either. Since both birth parents died long before I uncovered their identities, I never got to meet either one of them. I do know that my birth mother, Jackie, worked for Doc. And I have her coworker Conrad's recollection that she and Doc went out together a couple of times. But I will never know exactly how their apparent personal relationship started or ended.

The best news, of course, was that both of my biological families had welcomed and accepted me.

After twenty-five years of knowing Mike, my mother's first son, we had become real brothers. Now I had another brother, Doug, and a new sister, Elaine. Someday, I hoped I would be as close to them as I was to Mike.

Just to play it safe, I decided to wait until the full reports were in my hands before I shared the results. When they did come in, I examined each table closely. I could see exactly why the extra markers made three scores go down and two scores go up.

The reports also listed a percentage for each combination. It was the calculated probability that each man was my half sibling:

Doug	87.4 percent
Vern	59.8 percent
Joe	55.7 percent
Dale	34.2 percent
Dave	4.6 percent

Naturally, I would have preferred a 100 percent confirmation. But understanding how this test worked, I realized that a completely definitive answer was not possible. This was as good as I could do with then-current technology.

Sure, there was still a 13 percent chance that Doug was not my half sibling. But knowing that Jackie went out with Doc and he was then prone to extramarital affairs, I felt comfortable with the conclusion.

The first person I decided to call with the news was Doug. He was, after all, the first-place finisher in the "Win-a-Brother Contest."

Doug told me he was not surprised. He'd had a hunch all along that Doc would prove to be my biological father.

"It just made sense since she worked for him and they were known to have gone out together."

"My guess," I said, "is that Jackie never told him she was pregnant. She just quit her job and left town. She may have honestly thought that Conrad was the father of her child. Or she did not want to risk this affair with a married man becoming public."

"I'm sure you're right," Doug said. "If my father had known, he would have taken care of his responsibility just like Uncle Vernie did with Vern. That's the kind of men they were."

"I need to send you a check for my DNA test," Doug continued.

"That won't be necessary," I replied. "No one else paid for their test and I can't think of any reason why you should. I'm just thankful that you pushed me to include you."

Doug said he would pass on the news to his sister, Elaine. He also gave me her phone number so I could call later and introduce myself.

My next call was to Dale. The only boy in his family, he had been looking forward to having a brother. He was disappointed in the results, but I managed to cheer him up.

"At this stage in our lives," I said, "there really isn't much difference between a half brother and a cousin. We're still family and where we go with our relationship is up to us."

When I notified Joe, he said it was a good outcome for me.

"Uncle Doc was my favorite uncle. He was the glue that kept the family together."

Dave congratulated me. He described Doc as being in overdrive with lots of energy and ambition.

"I remember Uncle Doc once had a Cadillac with the horns of a bull mounted on the front."

I smiled at the image. It was the classic stereotype of a Texas rancher.

Then I called Vern, the earlier surprise addition to the family. He said he only met Doc once…and it was just a couple months before the man died.

"I was working at an Austin restaurant when Doc came in and asked for me. He introduced himself, his wife, and the man with them. I did not recognize the other man, but a coworker informed me that it was the attorney general of Texas."

Doc knew people in high places.

Gerry, my supporter from day one, was mildly disappointed in the outcome. "I was kind of hoping my father was the one," she said. "I enjoy having Vern as a brother and I wanted you to be my brother, too."

Now that the DNA test had pointed strongly to Doc as my father, she had something for me. The next time we met, Gerry presented me with a cowboy hat.

"Uncle Doc forgot this on one of his trips to Michigan and I was unable to return it before he died. I want you to have it."

I was thrilled to have something that belonged to my birth father. Besides being a personal item, the big hat was an instant reminder of Texas, where my paternal ancestry had been firmly rooted since 1859.

Trying the hat on, I was amazed to find it a perfect fit. Although Doc and I did not look a lot alike, at least we shared the same hat size.

I did not call Dale's mother, Mattie, since Dale was going to tell her the results. Though she never admitted it, the thought of her Wayne being my father must have bothered her. I later heard that she was relieved by the new result.

Adding up all the names I had encountered over the last few months, I counted two siblings and at least twelve cousins. Since most lived in Texas, Pat and I quickly agreed on what to do next.

We were going to Texas.

42

JOURNEY

In late October 2007, less than four weeks after the revised sibling DNA test positioned Doc as my birth father, Pat and I headed south. We were going to visit my new siblings and as many cousins as possible.

First, we drove from Michigan to Kentucky and spent two nights with Pat's brother. From his place it was only a four-hour drive to Cousin Vern's home in Alabama. We had already met Vern and his wife at the Richards reunion, but we looked forward to seeing them again.

Upon our arrival, we were pleased to discover that Vern's wife was a gourmet cook. She fed us a fabulous dinner.

Vern told us what it had been like to discover his own family's secret: that his biological father was Vernie Richards and not his mother's husband. He also showed us a photo of Livonia Boy, a highly successful racehorse Vernie had owned. Another prized possession was a textbook on industrial geography that Vernie had authored while teaching at the Henry Ford Trade School.

The next morning we said our good-byes and Pat and I drove farther south to meet one of Dale's sisters at a restaurant near her home. Another Alabama resident, she turned out to be a charming lady. We were sorry we couldn't spend more time with her. But she had to return to work and we had a lot of miles to cover that day.

From there, we turned west and drove the rest of the day, stopping for the night at a small town in Louisiana. The following afternoon we found our way to Cousin Dale's ranch in East Texas. Located in a region known as The Piney Woods, Dale's ranch looked more like Michigan than the vast plains I had imagined.

We stayed two nights with Dale and got to see how this rancher cared for his far-flung herds of cattle. Moving from place to place in a large truck one day and an all-terrain vehicle the next, we watched in amazement as Dale walked fearlessly among the huge beasts. Knowing exactly why he was there, they rushed to consume the pellets of food he spread on the ground.

Not far from Dale's modern log home, he showed us the ruins of our great-grandfather's 1860-era cabin. Seeing the site provided a solid sense of place that had been missing from my family history.

Dale also took us to the local cemetery, the resting place of my father, Doc, and Dale's father, Wayne. Nearby were the headstones of our paternal grandparents and great-grandparents.

Due to his position on the local school board, Dale had to attend a political function for a couple hours. So he gave us directions to his mother's house out on the paved road.

Mattie was expecting us. Now that everyone had heard my father was Doc and not Mattie's husband, Wayne, the meeting was far more relaxed than what I once imagined it would be.

Then Dale's other sister—the one who had prepared the photo album of their family for me—stopped by for a brief introduction.

Wayne's premature death had left Mattie and her three children to run the ranch alone. A huge scrapbook told of Mattie's accomplishments, including various awards like "Rancher of the Year."

Dale was divorced and Mattie had invited Dale's ex-wife to meet us. When Dale returned from town, Mattie treated us all to a home-cooked Texan dinner.

The following day, Pat and I left the ranch and drove toward Houston to meet my cousin, Joe.

Joe introduced us to his wife and daughters at their home in an upscale suburb. Then he gave Pat and me an after-hours tour of his huge orthodontics office. We were impressed with the equipment, the décor, and all the little things Joe had thought of to make getting braces a positive experience for children and their parents.

Even though my rancher cousin, Dale, and my orthodontist cousin, Joe, had picked completely different careers, I could tell that each was an expert in his chosen field.

Joe and his wife took us out to a restaurant where Joe's younger brother, Greg, also a dentist, joined us for dinner and a long evening of storytelling.

The next day, Pat and I drove west to San Antonio. Joe's wife had baked a batch of wonderful cookies to take with us. Pat tries to avoid sweets, but I love them. So I naturally indulged myself and Pat eventually gave in to temptation.

We got a room on the famous San Antonio River Walk and became tourists for a day. While there, we toured a place I had wanted to visit since I was eight years old: the Alamo.

I was that young when Walt Disney glued me to my family's black-and-white television screen with his *Davy Crockett* series. The episode at the Alamo had a profound impact on my young mind. Unlike the heroes in my comic books and other childhood stories, the good guys lost this battle. Worse yet, they were all killed.

In case Walt Disney's version wasn't memorable enough, Hollywood had retold the story many more times in the following decades. I absolutely had to see the Alamo.

While browsing the museum shop, I found a book called *Heroes of the Alamo and Goliad.* Remembering that my second great-grand uncle had reportedly died at Goliad, I scanned the pages that listed the casualties. Sure enough, John Richards was listed among the Texas revolutionaries killed at Goliad.

Proudly, I bought the book.

We left San Antonio and drove north with two more big visits ahead of us: my brother, Doug, and my sister, Elaine.

219

Once more, we noticed a dichotomy similar to the one in East Texas. Doug lived way out in the country with horses, dogs, and chickens, while Elaine's address was in the suburbs of a small city.

We visited Doug and his wife first and received a warm greeting. It was soon obvious that my brother and I were both quiet men who would wait patiently for our turn to talk. Our more outgoing wives liked each other immediately and seemed to carry 90 percent of the conversation. I wondered if Doug and I would ever get to speak one on one.

The chance came at dinner when Doug took us and some of his extended family to a Mexican restaurant. As he and I sat at one end of a long table, Doug told me about our father and his life before and after Dann's Tavern.

Doug described Doc as a serial entrepreneur. In his lifetime, he was involved in more than forty diverse businesses. Bars and nightclubs were a big part of the story. But other ventures included a soft-serve ice cream franchise, a pig farm, a movie theater, and a collection of retail stores. Although some businesses were failures, Doc had enough successes to ultimately get into ranching.

Doug was three years older than I was. Like his father before him, he was part businessman and part rancher. His home included a barn with horses and a pony for his grandchildren.

His primary ranch was quite a distance from where he was currently living, so we did not get to see it on that trip. But like Cousin Dale, Doug obviously loved the land and the ranching life of his ancestors.

When we returned from dinner, Doug called two of his adult children and had me speak to them on the phone. When he introduced me as their uncle, I knew I was accepted.

With everyone else gone, the four of us talked long into the night about many things, including my long search and the DNA testing that had brought us together.

In the morning, after a farm-fresh breakfast provided by their chickens, we said good-bye and drove north to meet my sister, Elaine.

I had already found one brother, Mike, on my birth mother's side. So I was completely at ease with having a second brother on my birth father's side. But what would it be like to have a sister? I had no idea.

During my teenage years, close relationships with girls my age meant dating. Since meeting Pat at age twenty, all my other close friends had been male. I had female coworkers, of course, but those relationships revolved around work.

Elaine was excited to meet us. When we sat down in her living room, she began talking as if she had known us forever. She explained that this home was temporary. Recently divorced, she was having her former home remodeled to make it more saleable.

This home didn't look temporary to me. It was extensively decorated and unmistakably feminine. She noted that she had designed and decorated the other home to fit her unique taste.

"I need to de-Elaine it," she explained, "so more people will like it."

Elaine's friendly, forthright manner made us comfortable and eased a lot of my concerns. Comparing birth dates, we discovered that my sister was just three months younger than I was—an odd circumstance made possible because of our different mothers.

While Doug had filled me in on Doc's business life, Elaine told us more about the man as a husband and father. Like everyone else, he was not perfect. But his overall temperament reminded me in some ways of myself.

Elaine, Doc's only daughter, had married young, ultimately bearing five daughters of her own. She was now thrilled to have grandchildren.

Her youngest daughter and the daughter's boyfriend were nearby, so we all met for lunch at a restaurant. Enjoying our time together, Pat and I hung around much longer than planned. But now we had to begin our long drive back to Michigan.

◆

Over the next two and a half days, Pat and I had plenty of time to reflect. We concluded that our journey to Texas had been the perfect capstone to the bigger journey of my search for biological roots.

Twenty-six years earlier, I had begun my search, looking for a brother and the truth about my birth mother. Eventually, I discovered both.

Neither Mike nor I had known much about our mother, due to her premature death and my adoption. But my search had taught both of us a lot about her.

The product of two alcoholic parents and a broken home, Jackie had spent three years of her late childhood living in a Salvation Army home. From there, every year of her life was remarkably eventful.

- At fifteen, she returned to her mother's home, only to find a stepfather she couldn't stand.
- At sixteen, she quit school to marry her best friend's older brother.
- At seventeen, she gave birth to her first son, Mike.
- At eighteen, having left her abusive husband, she placed Mike with his grandmother.
- At nineteen, she got pregnant a few months before her divorce was final.
- At twenty, she gave birth to her second son, giving me up for adoption.
- At twenty-one, she and her younger sister died from the trauma of a Jeep accident.

Jackie never gave up on her dream of getting Mike back and making a home for him. From the time she left Mike's father to the day of her death, she always worked two jobs: a manufacturing job during the week and a waitressing job on the weekends.

The exception was the last five months of her pregnancy when she lived with my adoptive parents in Lansing. Yet even then, she washed hair in Mom's beauty shop.

For the last two years of her life, Jackie took advantage of her good looks and popularity to date many guys and do a lot of partying. I'll never know exactly why she got involved with a married man. Perhaps it was because most of the young, single men were off fighting a war.

Now that I had met my new siblings, I felt my search was over. I was now enjoying the fruits of discovering another new family.

"I'm a lucky man," I said. "Most people are only blessed with two parents. I had four. Two of them created me from the DNA of my biological ancestors. And the other two molded me into the person I am today."

"And now you have four families in your life instead of two," Pat added.

"Yes," I said. "Best of all, I don't have to give up anybody in my adopted family. It's not an either-or thing. I'm just adding on."

Pat's next comment summarized my feelings exactly. "You can't have too much family," she said.

Nearing home, we began to reminisce about the incredible maze I had passed through to get to this point, including all the false information and dead-end leads.

"The one rumor that never made any sense," I noted, "was the one about my mother being a nurse and my father being a Lansing doctor. I could never identify the source or explain how they got it so wrong."

"Wasn't the woman who put your parents in touch with your birth mother a nurse?" Pat asked.

"Yes," I replied. "I could see that part of the story getting distorted into my mother *being* a nurse. But why on earth would someone think my father was a doctor?"

In an instant, some previously unrelated thoughts converged in my brain.

"Wait a minute," I exclaimed. "Even though my birth father's given name was Douglas, those close to him called him Doc!"

Jackie, who worked with him for months, could have known him by that name. And she lived with my adoptive parents for five whole months before I was born. Could she have slipped just one time and referred to her baby's father as Doc?

Perhaps Dad misconstrued her remark and proudly told a friend that I was the son of a doctor. Since my parents lived in Lansing, the rumor about my birth father being a Lansing doctor could have developed from there.

This was only speculation, of course. Like other missing details, the source of that rumor would remain a mystery. But at least I had identified my birth father.

Or so I thought.

43

MISSION

My words to Dale that "there really isn't much difference between a half brother and a cousin" proved to be an accurate assessment.

Having gotten to know so many family members during the long, confusing wait for sibling test results, I felt just as close to my Richards cousins as I did my Richards siblings.

As one would expect, actual face time proved to be more dependent on geography than our precise relationship. Pat and I saw more of cousins Gerry and David, who lived in Michigan, than family members a thousand miles away in Texas.

We did make periodic return trips to the Lone Star state. And some of the Texas people, most reliably Dale, journeyed to Michigan for the annual Richards reunion.

In 2010, Pat and I had the privilege of hosting the reunion at our home. More than anything else, that made us feel like part of the family.

On my birth mother's side, my brother, Mike, and I had now known each other almost half our lives. It did not seem possible. He was still in Tennessee, but we got together at his place or ours on a roughly annual basis.

Aunt Lynn's health declined steadily and she died early in 2010. Pat and I drove across the state to pay our respects and got to reconnect briefly with cousins on my maternal side.

The older generation of my adoptive family had already passed away by the time I found both of my birth families. So I have no idea what they would have thought of my new relationships. But the cousins I had known all my life were intrigued and supportive.

There's no question that DNA testing played a huge role in my search. Yet I was surprised to discover that most adoptees and many genealogists were still unaware of genetic genealogy.

By 2008, I decided that sharing what I had learned would be my personal mission. For more than thirty years, I had worked in marketing communications—writing about my clients' technical products and services. So I felt well prepared to write about the world of DNA testing.

That summer I began slowly to build a web site, which I registered as **DNA-Testing-Adviser.com**. I was still doing a lot of client work, so it was 2009 before I had sufficient content to attract even a small number of visitors.

After learning that my biological father was a Richards, I had joined the Richards DNA Surname Project at Family Tree DNA. When the volunteer project administrator decided to step down in January 2009, she asked me to take over the project, which I did.

Once I was on the administrator list, I learned that Family Tree DNA hosted an annual conference for project administrators in its headquarters city of Houston. Since my Richards family had lived just outside Houston since 1859, I thought this was an interesting coincidence.

The 2009 conference was scheduled for March, just two months away. I tried to register and discovered that all the spaces had been filled. Determined to learn more about DNA testing directly from these experts, I wrote the company and reported my successful use of its Y-DNA test to uncover the surname of my birth father.

They somehow made room for me and let me attend the conference.

Even better, they asked if I could stop by their office and tell my story in front of a video camera. I did that and got to meet the company's founder and president, Bennett Greenspan. The video that developed from that interview eventually was added to the Family Tree DNA web site.

I had placed a feedback form on my own web site so people could contact me with questions and comments. A few weeks after the Houston conference, a science reporter from *The Wall Street Journal* used that form to contact me.

He had heard about me from Bennett. After visiting my web site, he wanted to tell my story. He interviewed me several times by phone and on May 2, 2009, his article appeared on the front page of *The Wall Street Journal.*

The newspaper included several photos that I had provided. Heavily edited to fit the space available, the final version got a few details wrong. Yet I was thrilled with the coverage. It also appeared in the online edition and my web site traffic took its first significant upward spike.

A few weeks later, our local newspaper, the *Grand Rapids Press*, asked for an interview. When I agreed, they sent a reporter and a photographer to our home. That article also received front-page coverage. Since both of my fathers were featured in the story, it was fitting that the article ran on Father's Day.

While the newspaper articles were lengthy, I knew that 90 percent of the story remained untold. The idea of writing a book began to percolate in my brain.

Still, I knew I couldn't recall the whole story without a laborious dive into my huge collection of notes, documents, and correspondence going back almost thirty years. I didn't think I could find the time to even do that, let alone write an entire book.

In 2010, the Great Recession—which hit Michigan especially hard—provided the opportunity.

I had three consulting clients at the time and two of them slashed the marketing budgets that paid for my services. For the first time in my adult life, I suddenly had significant free time.

I jumped into the book project.

Meanwhile, I began receiving invitations to speak in front of genealogy and civic groups around Grand Rapids. I discovered that even people who were not adoptees or genealogists were fascinated by my story.

I continued to follow advancements in genetic genealogy, taking additional DNA tests and writing about them on my web site.

In late 2009, I learned about a new DNA test from a company called 23andMe. Although the company focused on health testing, it wanted genealogists to test a new feature called Relative Finder. I signed up to be a beta tester, which is someone a company uses to test a new product to find and work out any potential bugs.

Like the sibling test I took in 2007, this test looked at the "autosomal" DNA passed down from both parents. But unlike the old sibling test, which only compared people on fifteen markers, this test checked hundreds of thousands of locations, looking for long strings of identical DNA.

And unlike the Y-DNA test that told me my birth father's surname, this test could be taken by women as well as men...and if two people match, the common ancestor could be from *any* branch of their family trees.

My closest early match was with a woman predicted to be a third cousin. By contacting her and comparing our lines, I was able to pinpoint our common ancestor. She and I are actually third cousins once removed on my paternal side.

This was extremely cool. Immediately, I could foresee male and female adoptees using this test to find biological relatives from their birth families.

As time went on, however, it became clear that hosting this genealogy feature at a health-testing company was less than ideal.

The presence of genetic health data requires extremely high privacy walls around each user. Furthermore, most 23andMe users are secretive as well, preferring to be anonymous on Relative Finder. These factors create formidable barriers to communication.

For example, you can only invite your matches to discuss your ancestral connections by going through an internal communication system that enforces the rigid privacy protections.

In addition, you can only see the details of a match—i.e. where you match on individual chromosomes—if that person specifically agrees to share his or her genome with you.

The company was marketing the test aggressively, so the number of matches I had kept growing. Yet most of my matches never responded to my inquiries. And those who did usually were not genealogists and had limited knowledge of their family trees.

Fortunately, a few months after Relative Finder was introduced, Family Tree DNA launched a similar test called Family Finder. It employed the same basic technology that Relative Finder used. Yet it had one critically important difference: it neither collected nor analyzed any health data.

So I became a beta tester for Family Finder, as well.

Like other genetic genealogy tests at Family Tree DNA, Family Finder was created with genealogists in mind. Instead of operating within a medical system strangled by confidentiality, users interact in a far more open culture designed for easy sharing. Both DNA results and genealogical data can be readily compared.

As soon as you get a match, you can see that person's name and e-mail address. You can contact him or her at any time and even attach files related to your family tree.

Plus, you can immediately explore the details of your matches with several people at a time through a clever tool called the Chromosome Browser. You don't have to wait for people to accept your "sharing invitation."

Thoughtfully, Family Tree DNA also included other features in Family Finder to support the exploration of matches, such as automated surname matching and even the display of genealogical pedigrees.

Without the added draw of health testing, Family Finder appeals to a more limited audience than Relative Finder. So you don't get as many matches. But nearly all of my matches responded to my inquiries and had extensive family trees.

Over time, a remarkable feature of these two new tests became apparent: both Family Finder and Relative Finder proved to be far better than the old sibling tests for confirming close relationships.

The sibling tests only spot check a handful of markers and then *calculate* the probability of two people having a certain relationship.

These new tests, on the other hand, compare huge regions on your chromosomes and actually *measure* the amount of DNA two people have in common.

For first cousins and closer, the tests are breathtakingly conclusive.

I didn't know it at the time, but my story was about to take another dramatic turn.

44

NOT AGAIN

My own DNA was already in the Relative Finder and Family Finder databases. So I began to wonder...maybe I should retest some of my Richards relatives to corroborate the earlier finding that Doc was my birth father.

Unfortunately, these new tests were still priced at a few hundred dollars each. While both labs were well aware of my web site, neither one was sending me any free test kits. I would have to pay retail, just like everyone else.

In my mind, I couldn't justify the expense when I still believed that my case was settled. The 87 percent probability of Doug being my half brother was a more positive result than what I was hearing from others who wrote to me about their sibling tests.

Most people in the Family Finder and Relative Finder databases are not trying to confirm a relationship with a close relative. Nearly everyone in Family Finder and a fraction of those in Relative Finder are genealogists.

They are using these tests to find distant, previously unknown relatives in their family trees. People who share segments above a certain size almost certainly descend from a common ancestor. If you compare family trees with the people you match, you may be able to discover who that common ancestor was and then expand or at least confirm that branch of your family tree.

Over time, as serious genealogists continued to explore Family Finder and Relative Finder, it became clear that there was a genealogical advantage to testing multiple family members.

For example, if you and a relative on your paternal side both take one of these tests, the people who match both of you are more likely to be connected through your father's family. By focusing your efforts on that side of your tree, you may be able to determine the common ancestor more quickly.

Family Finder even provides a filter to let you quickly see which of your matches are "in common with" any particular match. On Relative Finder, finding common matches is a manual process, but it's still doable if you have access to both people's data.

By the fall of 2011, I decided that I could no longer ignore this development and be faithful to my web site readers. If I was going to tell people how to take advantage of multiple relative testing, I had to explore the process myself.

I decided to bite the bullet and order another test kit from each lab. Then I had to choose one relative to take each test.

Since my cousin Vern's wife had done the early genealogy work on the Richards family, I figured they would enjoy working with me on our family tree. I asked Vern to take the 23andMe test and he agreed.

For the Family Finder kit, I decided to ask my sister, Elaine. I had sensed that she felt left out when I was testing Doug on the sibling test. So I called and explained what I wanted. She was pleased to be asked and agreed to take the new test.

Vern sent in his sample immediately after receiving the test kit. Elaine happened to be in the process of moving when her kit arrived. She slipped it into a packing box where it lay hidden for weeks.

This meant that Vern's results came in well ahead of Elaine's. After receiving a notification by e-mail that his results were ready, I logged into to my 23andMe account to check my Relative Finder matches.

I could see my relationship to each matching person based on the number of segments we shared and the total amount of shared DNA. My closest prior match had been with the previously mentioned third cousin. She and I shared three segments and had less than 1 percent of our DNA in common.

The amount of DNA that people share on this test depends on their relationship. A parent and child or two full siblings will share about 50 percent.

At the next step down, there are three relationships that share about 25 percent:

- grandparent and grandchild
- aunt/uncle and nephew/niece
- half siblings

First cousins, the next closely related group, will share around 12.5 percent. That's where I assumed Vern and I would be. But when I looked at Vern's data, I could not believe my eyes. Vern and I shared 32 segments and 22 percent of our DNA!

At 22 percent, we were clearly in the 25 percent ballpark...and the only relationship that fit the facts of our situation was half siblings.

The startling new conclusion was inescapable. Since we had different mothers, Vern and I must have shared the same father.

Vern had always been recognized as Vernie's son. So that implied that my father was Vernie instead of Doc!

I was dumbfounded.

The earlier sibling test had calculated an 87 percent probability that Doc was my father and only a 60 percent probability that Vernie was my father. I had based my original conclusion on the larger index number and the higher probability. Knowing that Doc had been my mother's employer had also supported that conclusion.

Yet the sibling test results were still only estimates from a tiny number of markers—just fifteen to be exact. What looked like the more probable conclusion in 2007 now had been proven wrong by an actual measurement of 700,000 markers.

Clearly, the idea of Vernie being my father did make sense. Vernie fit my longstanding image of a tall, dark-haired father. People said I looked more like Vernie than Doc. And Vernie's brown eyes were a more understandable match for me than Doc's problematic blue eyes.

Nevertheless, I realized there was one other possibility. Perhaps Doc had a secret relationship with Vern's mother and was the father to four of us: Doug, Elaine, Vern, and me.

I picked up the phone and called Vern.

After explaining the test results, I asked for his reaction. Vern was fine with the idea of us being siblings. Although he had been told that Vernie was his father, he could not rule out the possibility that his mother may also have slept with Doc.

Since she was now deceased, it was too late to ask her. And that was not a conversation Vern would have liked to have anyway.

I told Vern that Elaine would also be taking one of these new tests. We both realized that her results would either confirm or eliminate Doc as our biological father.

There was no doubt that Elaine enjoyed having me as another brother. So I knew she would be disappointed if I had to revise that conclusion. But with Vern now confirmed as my half sibling, Elaine could not be my sister unless Doc had fathered all of us.

Yet if that were the case, Gerry would lose Vern as her brother.

Weeks passed and the whole issue hung like the Sword of Damocles over my head. All along, I had two simple goals. I wanted to know the truth about my birth and I didn't want to hurt anybody.

Now I found myself caught between the proverbial rock and a hard place. Somebody would be hurt no matter what the truth turned out to be.

A few days before Christmas in 2011, I received an e-mail from Family Tree DNA that Elaine's results were ready. Anxiously, I logged in and checked my Family Finder Matches.

There was Elaine's name. I held my breath and looked at the data. Family Finder does not report the number of shared segments or the percent of shared DNA like Relative Finder does. Instead, this test reports the total length of all the blocks we share and the length of the longest block.

Elaine and I were right in the heart of the first-cousin range.

Confirming Elaine as a first cousin eliminated her father, Doc from being my father too. Now it looked like I finally knew the real truth. Somehow, Doc's older brother Vernie, owner of the Joy Bar, had been intimate with my birth mother, Jackie.

While I was glad to know the truth, I did not yet feel like celebrating.

My family and I had lived with the false conclusion that Doc was my father for more than four years. And prior to that, there was the tentative conclusion that Dale's father, Wayne, had been my father.

I had to retract that first conclusion and now I was facing a more shocking retraction.

All of the branches of my family plus countless friends and genealogy contacts had heard my story. Plus, thousands of strangers had read about it on my web site, *The Wall Street Journal*, and the *Grand Rapids Press*.

Now I knew the ending of that story was flat-out wrong. Doc was not my birth father. I had unknowingly misled myself and everyone else.

Naturally, I shared this news and my feelings with Pat. She tried to reassure me that I had taken the best DNA test available in 2007 and had drawn the most logical conclusion. I had not tried to mislead anybody.

When this didn't cheer me, she suggested a plan of action that had not occurred to me: "Maybe you should just keep your mouth shut."

45

ONE FINAL DECISION

Pat's reasoning was simple. My goal of knowing the truth was complete. Vernie was my birth father. I could accomplish my second goal of not hurting anyone simply by keeping quiet about these new findings.

"You often say that there is not much practical difference between a half sibling and a first cousin," Pat argued. "You could just let everyone else go on believing that Doc was your father. Then nothing changes and no one gets hurt."

Pat explained that she was especially concerned about Doc's daughter, Elaine, who she felt would be hurt by losing the new brother she had been so pleased to discover.

We did not have long to talk this out. On the following day, Pat's sister and her family flew in from California to spend the Christmas holidays with us.

After everyone left, I realized that Vern already knew about his test results and knew that Elaine was being tested. There was no way I could keep him in the dark.

I called Vern and filled him in. He was relieved that Gerry was still his sister. From his point of view, he had added a new brother without making any waves that could hurt anyone.

Vern had discussed the new DNA tests with his wife but had not told anyone else. I explained Pat's idea of not sharing this with others and asked him to continue keeping it quiet unless he heard differently from me. He agreed.

"I understand your situation," Vern said. "I'm just glad you have to make that decision and not me."

New Year's Day fell on a Sunday and several bowl games were on TV the next day. I lost myself in football for awhile, especially an exciting Outback Bowl where my Michigan State Spartans beat the Georgia Bulldogs in triple-overtime.

As the glow of victory drained away, my DNA problem quickly returned to the forefront of my brain. I kept weighing the imagined consequences of telling everyone versus the idea of burying these new results forever.

Pat and I agonized over this for a few more days. Then on the following weekend, we reached a decision.

We simply could not go on, year after year, interacting with my newest family and letting them think that Doc was my father. It would be a lie. And we would know it was a lie even if others did not.

Furthermore, I had spent decades getting around lies and cover-ups, being repeatedly shocked at the family secrets parents hid from their children. I could not engage in a cover-up of my own.

I had to tell everyone and let the chips fall where they might.

First on my list was Elaine, since it was her DNA test that eliminated Doc as my father. I tried to reach her a couple times by phone, but she did not answer.

Anxious to get started before I chickened out, I decided to call her brother, Doug. I reached him on the first try and carefully explained the powerful new DNA tests and my surprising results from testing Vern and Elaine.

By now, I knew Doug to be the epitome of laid back. Nothing ever seemed to bother him. As I expected, he accepted this news gracefully.

Doug had heard enough about the family's early days in the bar business to explain how Jackie and Vernie must have known each other. First of all, Doc and Vernie were frequently at each other's bars. In addition, whenever a waitress at one bar was sick, a girl from the other bar would often be called in to take her shift.

That reminded me of a comment made by Jackie's best friend, Cordie, who also worked at Doc's bar. She said that everybody knew both brothers. Now I could clearly see why. And "everybody" certainly would have included Jackie.

While the conversation with Doug was an easy one, I suspected my talks with the female family members might not go nearly as well.

When I did reach Elaine, it was indeed a more difficult conversation. She had really enjoyed the thrill of discovering a new brother. Now she was disappointed to discover we were actually cousins. Once again, I found myself making the case that the precise relationship did not matter much at this stage of our lives.

My next call was to Gerry. She had been the first family member I found. Open to all possibilities, she had supported me throughout the process of recruiting family members to do the sibling test.

When those test results finally pointed to Doc as my father, she had expressed a little disappointment that it had not been her father, Vernie. So I was hoping she would accept this new finding as good news.

She did not.

First of all, Gerry challenged the results. She thought the sibling test had proved Doc was my father. How could this new test prove otherwise?

I tried to explain the difference. The sibling test just checked fifteen DNA markers from each son and then used some statistical formulas to calculate the probability that each man was my half sibling. Doug had the highest probability of 87 percent. But Vern had the second highest probability of 60 percent.

While Doug had been statistically more likely to be my half sibling, that conclusion was still a *guess*.

Never expecting a better DNA test to become available, I drew a conclusion based on the sibling tests and the circumstantial evidence that Doc was Jackie's employer and, therefore, the two had the greatest opportunity of entering into an intimate relationship.

With all of us anxious for an answer, I had allowed "probable" to morph into "proof." But I had been wrong.

I explained how the new Family Finder and Relative Finder tests compare two people on 700,000 markers. They look for long blocks of DNA that are identical in both of us. Those long blocks had to come from a common ancestor and the more long blocks we share, the closer the common ancestor must have been.

These new tests don't guess. They measure.

Finally accepting my argument that the new tests were better than the old test, Gerry surprised me with her next comments.

"I have always had a hard time believing that your father was the short, blue-eyed Doc," she exclaimed. "I thought you looked more like my dad and his brother, Joe."

Sometime earlier, I had printed the initial draft of my book for family members to read. Fortunately, I had not yet published it with the erroneous conclusion. Yet something I wrote in that draft had caught Gerry's eye.

"Do you remember the part in your book where you learned that your birth mother had named you Gerald? You never found any explanation for that."

"Yes," I agreed.

"My full name is Geraldine and I was five years old when you were born. Do you suppose Jackie saw me sometime or at least heard about me from my dad and liked my name?"

"When she got pregnant, Jackie thought about Geraldine as a girl's name…but when she had a boy, she named you Gerald."

That remark hit me like a ton of bricks. Once again, I had not put two and two together. The Geraldine-to-Gerald idea made a lot of sense.

Did Jackie just like the name, I wondered, or did she choose it because she knew Vernie was my father?

Then Gerry surprised me again: "I think you should test me on the new DNA test."

I explained that, logically, it wasn't necessary. A comparison of Elaine and me showed we were first cousins. That eliminated Elaine's father, Doc, as my father. A comparison of Vern and me showed we were half siblings. He and I must have had the same father and Vernie had publicly admitted being Vern's father.

Admittedly, the high cost also made me reluctant to order yet another test. But I didn't say anything about that.

"I don't care about the logic," Gerry pressed. "I will feel better if you test me and it proves we are half siblings."

This reminded me of the time when I tried to omit Doug from the sibling test due to his father's blue eyes and he insisted on being included.

Now it occurred to me that if Doug had been left out, Vern would have been my closest match and I would have stumbled into the correct answer four years ago.

"What if I split the cost of the test with you?" Gerry continued. I briefly protested, but she insisted on doing the test and paying for half of it.

That night I went online and ordered another Family Finder test for Gerry. In a couple days, her check arrived in the mail. She also enclosed copies of Vernie's obituaries and some previously unshared photos of her father and his brother, Joe, who she still thought looked the most like me.

Over the next few weeks, we exchanged a flurry of e-mails.

I could tell this was stressing her out and I felt badly about that. In one message she wrote, "I sure thought this puzzle was completed, but it sounds like we are starting all over again."

Gerry had long accepted the fact that her father had gotten Vern's mother pregnant in 1951. Vernie had openly wanted a son and Gerry's mother had refused to have any more children. Knowing that fact, the whole family had eventually given him a pass on that extramarital relationship.

An affair in 1945, however, would be an entirely different story. Gerry had trouble believing that the father she idolized could have been unfaithful to her mother that much earlier.

"I have mixed feelings about this whole thing," she wrote in an e-mail. "On one hand, I like the idea of you being a half brother, since I think you and Pat are a fantastic addition to the Richards family. On the other hand, I have to face that my Dad, who I thought at that time was a wonderful family man, did this to our happy little family."

Gerry even quoted Shakespeare: "The evil that men do lives after them. The good is oft interred with their bones."

As the reality began to sink in, however, Gerry began to cope with his apparent misconduct. "It probably was just a one-night fling," she wrote. "We all make mistakes at one time or another."

Then Gerry flipped back into denial, arguing that Jackie, who was only nineteen at the time, could not have been interested in a man twice her age.

On the other hand, I thought quietly to myself, a man of almost any age would have been attracted to a young woman as beautiful as Jackie was.

We soon spoke again by phone.

"I think she would have been more attracted to Joe," stated Gerry flatly. "He was only twenty-three and a good-looking Marine."

"Remember," I countered. "Joe had just been put on emergency leave due to battle fatigue. He probably wasn't that much fun to be around in August 1945."

Gerry and I continued our correspondence. At one point, she wrote that she once again felt like she was a character in a soap opera.

Fortunately, she still saw the bright side. "Oh well," she wrote. "It makes my life interesting!"

Eventually, we both reached the conclusion that our speculations were useless. We could not go back to 1945 and watch this soap opera unfold.

We would have to wait for the results of Gerry's DNA test.

46

CONFIRMATION

Over the following weeks, Gerry and I stayed in touch as we awaited her DNA test results. I saw signs that she was preparing herself for what now seemed inevitable.

"I will just have to accept whatever the outcome is," she wrote. "I keep reassuring myself that the results of this test will not change the way I feel about him. He was a sensational father to me and that is what I have to keep in mind."

In mid February, I received an e-mail from Family Tree DNA that Gerry's Family Finder test results were ready to view online. As I predicted, this high-tech comparison of her DNA with mine left no room for doubt.

Gerry was clearly my half sibling.

Family Tree DNA had recently added the capability to transfer DNA results from Relative Finder into Family Finder. Wanting to see everyone's results in one place, I had immediately ordered the transfer for Vern.

When Vern's results appeared in Family Finder, everything became perfectly clear. Vern, Gerry, and I were all half siblings to each other and Elaine was a first cousin to each of us.

No question about it. Vernie Fletcher Richards was my birth father.

I then used Family Finder's Chromosome Browser to see a graph of our common segments on individual chromosome pairs. This made the conclusion visually obvious.

When I called Gerry with the complete results, she was actually excited.

"I do not think you could have picked a better person than Vernie to be your dad," she exclaimed. "He was the greatest person in my life and loved me unconditionally. Congratulations...little brother!"

Gerry continued, "This has not changed my love and respect for my dad. As you know, we were extremely close and he was the most fantastic father and my hero."

"What I do feel bad about," she continued, "is that *our* dad did not even have a clue about you. He would have been thrilled to have such a wonderful son."

I was both relieved and delighted by Gerry's words. Now I felt that I had achieved both of my objectives. I had finally—and at long last—solved all the major mysteries surrounding my birth...and in the end, no one got seriously hurt.

Even Gerry's husband, who had once warned her about digging up old bones, was happy for Gerry and me. He had known Vernie as a great family man who took wonderful care of his family. He reminded Gerry that Vernie's involvement with my mother was no reflection on us in any way.

Gerry even complimented Jackie.

"I have to give your mom credit for not blaming my dad and breaking up our happy home. She must have suffered a lot of stress and decided in the end to do what was best for you. It was a big sacrifice on her part."

Yes, I thought, Jackie did a wonderful thing for Gerry by keeping quiet about Vernie. And placing me with Harold and Thelma Hill had been Jackie's ultimate gift to me.

As for the circumstances of her relationship with Vernie, we will never know for sure. But in all my research, I never heard anyone express even a hint of an affair between them.

The timing of my conception, just days after V-J Day, had always suggested a one-time celebratory encounter. Now, the good things I was hearing about Vernie as a family man certainly supported that theory.

For Gerry, the excitement that followed V-J Day was actually her earliest childhood memory. Just four years old, she remembered being in her yard and clutching the family dog that was frightened by all the fireworks being shot off around them.

Gerry and I were certain that Vernie never knew about me. On the other hand, we both had become convinced that Jackie knew Vernie had been my father.

"In my mind," she went on, "I think Jackie named you Gerald as a tie-in to Vernie."

Independently, I had reached the same conclusion. Concerned about losing custody of her son, Mike, over this encounter with a married man, Jackie had named a single man, Conrad, as my father.

Yet even though Conrad recently had proposed to her, she did not take the easy way out and simply become his wife. She chose not to tell him about her pregnancy, instructed her friends not to tell him, and left town to live with my adoptive parents.

I think she knew the baby she carried was not Conrad's. And when I was born, she intended "Gerald" to be a tiny clue for me and my descendents.

Yet even that clue was buried when my new parents rejected Gerald and re-named me Richard. If my search angel, Jeanette, had not uncovered Gerald as my original name and Gerry had not pointed out the similarity to Geraldine, I never would have caught the connection.

245

Gerry and I promptly arranged our first meeting as brother and sister. We picked the East Lansing suburb of Okemos as a convenient halfway spot and I suggested a chain restaurant that offered a free Wi-Fi connection. That would allow me to show her our DNA test results online.

Once this was set, I realized that we would be meeting less than a half mile from the restaurant where Conrad and I ate lunch after having our blood drawn for the DNA paternity test. That was more than twenty years ago! How time had flown.

On the way to Okemos, I stopped and bought a bouquet of roses that I presented to Gerry. She in turn surprised me with two hand-tooled leather belts that had belonged to my birth father. The well-worn, everyday belt said "Jack" in the back and the still pristine belt he saved for dressing up said "Vernie."

After we ate lunch, I got out my laptop and took Gerry through the online accounts for the Relative Finder and Family Finder tests. I showed her exactly what I saw as I confirmed that Vernie was my birth father.

Gerry presented me with more photos that I could scan and save. She then told me more about Vernie's life and some of the good things he did for his extended family. That list included subsidizing his youngest brother, so Wayne could stay on the family ranch and take care of their aging parents.

After Vernie arrived in Michigan, he became a beloved instructor and basketball coach at the Henry Ford Trade School. Sixteen years later, he began his stint in the bar business by purchasing the Joy Bar. After selling that bar, he took over the Good Time Bar that he had originally purchased for his brother, Joe, to run.

In the last twenty-five years of his life, Vernie was a breeder of horses and made a good living from harness racing. He helped turn Livonia into a city and was a longtime member of the Rotary Club, once serving as its president. One of his favorite projects was helping crippled children ride horses.

Gerry also brought me a copy of an old audio tape where Vernie was practicing his speech for a reunion of Henry Ford Trade School alumni and staff.

After returning home, I listened eagerly to the tape and was pleased to hear my birth father's rich voice with a distinctive Texas drawl. He was a good speaker and delivered an inspiring, often humorous speech.

Thinking back, I realized my quest for biological roots began in 1981—a full five years before Vernie died.

Unfortunately, I never came close to meeting him. Thanks to lies, cover-ups, the sealed records, my personal distractions, and the misleading sibling test results, my search had lurched ahead and stalled repeatedly over thirty-one years.

Looking back, I do not regret a minute of it. While frustrating at times, my search proved to be a rich and rewarding experience. I uncovered the truth about my birth parents, acquired wonderful new siblings and cousins, and built a family tree for my descendants.

Along the way, I made many new friends and got to speak with people who knew and loved my birth parents. By learning so many details about them and their families, I felt like I really did travel back in time.

In addition, I gained a deeper appreciation for my adoptive parents and the enormous role they played in my life.

When people hear my story, they sometimes congratulate me for finding my "real" parents. I'm always quick to correct them.

Yes, my birth parents played their biological role and left traces of themselves and their ancestors in my DNA.

But my adoptive parents were the ones who were there for me day in and day out, year after year. They provided the love, support, encouragement, and endless patience I needed to become a fully functioning adult. Finding family taught me that my adoptive parents were just as much real parents as were my birth parents.

The experts talk about nature versus nurture. Both are critically important in determining who we are. The inherent truth for adoptees, however, is that these two factors came from four different people.

And many of us will never know peace until we know all the pieces.

A MESSAGE FROM THE AUTHOR

My hopes for this book are simple.

I want to inspire adoptees and others of unknown or uncertain parentage to try DNA testing. Use what you learned from my story and your path to success should be much shorter than mine.

I'm also hoping that birth parents will be motivated to be tested too, making it easier for their never-forgotten children or maybe their grandchildren to learn about them someday.

As genetic genealogy tests become ever more powerful and the databases get larger, the process of finding and reuniting lost families will only get easier.

For current information and specific recommendations, visit my web site at **DNA-Testing-Adviser.com**. You can use the feedback form on my site to ask me questions, comment on this book, or arrange a presentation for your genealogy, adoption search, or civic group.

If you, too, are looking for your genetic roots, I wish you great success in your search. I sincerely hope you have a happy ending similar to the one that I enjoyed.

ACKNOWLEDGEMENT: I wish to thank my good friends, John Krueger and Bill Murphy. These excellent writers reviewed my drafts chapter by chapter. Their honest and insightful feedback made this a better book.

Made in the USA
Charleston, SC
20 September 2015